CAPITALISM, SOCIALISM, AND DEMOCRACY

WHAT YOU NEED TO KNOW
FOR THE COMING ELECTION

THOMAS LEWELLEN

Capitalism, Socialism, and Democracy

First Edition: 2022

Printed in the United States of America

10 9 8 7 6 5 4 3 2 1

DEFIANCE **PRESS**
& PUBLISHING

ISBN-13: 978-1-955937-92-4 (paperback)
ISBN-13: 978-1-955937-10-8 (ebook)

Published by Defiance Press and Publishing, LLC

Bulk orders of this book may be obtained by contacting Defiance Press and Publishing, LLC. www.defiancepress.com.

Public Relations Dept. – Defiance Press & Publishing, LLC
281-581-9300
pr@defiancepress.com

Defiance Press & Publishing, LLC
281-581-9300
info@defiancepress.com

CONTENTS

INTRODUCTION

*"There is no perfect government, nor perfect economy,
nor institution, nor any man. The choice we must make
for the journey toward perfection is which road to take,
one of our own making or one of someone else's design."*
Tom Lewellen

THIS BOOK'S MISSION IS TO provide as leanly as possible a discussion of the benefits and liabilities of each ideology when coupled with Democracy. The intent isn't to write an unreadable, overly cited, peer-reviewed dissertation, but a simple straightforward analysis to give perspective to voters who attempt to unravel the non-stop propaganda regurgitated by the elites in the media, the academy and in politics. As Leonardo da Vinci recommended, "Simplicity is the Ultimate Sophistication." I hope to be short and sweet. Something easy to understand for *common* people like you and me. Actually, ingenious commoners may be a better term as this nation would not exist without our continuous ingenuity.

A Short History of the War Between the Ideologies

Joseph Schumpeter's *Socialism, Capitalism and Democracy,* published in 1942, could never be eclipsed by what follows in this book. His masterpiece is a fabulous endeavor that engineers a unique view of how an economy works. His book was and is a wonderful alternative to the economic debate stirred by Maynard Keynes's *The General Theory of Employment* and Joseph Hayek's *The Road to Serfdom.*

Keynesian economics perfectly aligned with 1930s politicians who coveted bigger, more involved government. Keynes's econometrics and money-multipliers are central to his theory that government could borrow large sums of money to employ workers in non-productive jobs producing full employment. Today, Keynes's thinking shows up in 'stimulus' proposals to 'prime' the economy for growth during a recession. This big government, centrally-planned, economic strategy led many to believe that Keynes was a

Socialist, as his thinking about spending has been pivotal to the Socialist approach in western nations. He was, however, an admitted Capitalist who had accumulated $30 million in wealth (2020 dollars) during his lifetime.

Hayek, on the other hand, thought Keynes's interventionist approach created too much central planning. Hayek was born of the Austrian School of Economics, a more liberal, yet traditional approach to open markets and free trade—a Capitalist approach. Politically, Keynes dominates in both parties. Republicans, though, trend toward Hayek.

Schumpeter created a third rail of economics which gained attention among twentieth century economists and policy makers, but was largely an afterthought, not the main meal. Schumpeter promoted entrepreneurs as a crucial component that drives a great economy, their new innovations being essential to the vast increases in productivity, economic growth, and wealth in the first few decades of the twentieth century. His theory purported that new disruptive ideas, inventions, and innovations were the cornerstone of economic success, the supply of which determines future economic growth. Though innovation has throughout history driven economic progress, during this century, innovation and especially disruptive innovation has been embraced by entrepreneurs, big business, and big government alike. No longer are business titans buying up entrepreneur's inventions to kill their ideas and protect the status quo; they are seeking innovation they cannot otherwise create on their own. This sea change in perspective is fundamental to America's future economic success.

The theories of Keynes, Hayek and Schumpeter align with the Socialist, Capitalist, and a new entrepreneurial approach to government. They are the guides to understanding today's two current political states of governance as well as a new innovative path forward. The objective of this book is to leverage what we have learned over the last century about the merits and benefits, as well as the challenges and liabilities, of Capitalism and Socialism to provide the reader with a shorter, more accessible comparison of both philosophies to make sense of political double-speak coming from Washington. I intend to address the shortcomings of the political marketing of Socialism versus Capitalism which has been a subtext during elections but never quite a public debate.

Over the last two decades, the media and political marketers have launched verbal missiles aimed to generate click bait to harm candidates of one ilk or another. Despite billions spent on marketing as well as the vast value of free media, nary a dollar has been spent to educate the voter about what each word means. My hope is to articulate the gulf between Socialist and Capitalist ideologies, thereby clarifying the difference between each political party's vastly different governing principles. The Democrats have adopted a Socialist *approach* (not quite full-blown Socialism) for policy formation, while the Republicans have adopted a Capitalist *approach* (not quite full-blown Capitalism.) Lastly, I will use this information to better understand our economic, social, and cultural competition with China for which America has yet to produce a plan or strategy for winning or even competing.

If there were ever a political campaign that should have debated the differences of Socialism versus Capitalism, 2020 was that campaign. Since FDR, there has not been a time that the Democrat and Republican economic principles have been so divergent. Though campaign advertising placed focus on Socialism versus Capitalism, not much more than sound bites and name-calling ensued. No meaningful discussion occurred regarding how each style of government might harm or help our nation. Socialism and Capitalism were used as hazy pejoratives. Being associated with either term diminished or enhanced one's brand ID depending upon the viewer's political affiliation.

The 2020 election results might lead us to believe that about half of us like the idea of Socialism and the other half likes Capitalism, as the vote tallies were close. The House and Senate races produced nearly even splits. The presidency was decided by less than 100,000 votes in four close state races. Polling suggests, however, that feelings about Socialism, outside of whom we voted for, are less desirable than Capitalism, but Capitalism did not rock poll numbers either. According to an NPR poll, respondents had a 28 percent favorable opinion of Socialism, with 58 percent unfavorable. Capitalism according to Pew Research is favored by 53 percent of respondents. Gallup dives deeper into the citizen's demographics stating that those over fifty-five years of age are decidedly pro capitalism—68 percent, while those under fifty-five favored Socialism by the same margin.

If the reader sought input from friends and colleagues about the definition of Socialism or Capitalism, answers were likely lean. *Socialism is where government does things for us. Capitalism is when banks invest in business. Capitalism makes rich people richer. Capitalism hurts income inequality. Socialism helps the poor people.* These definitions are not wrong so much as they are incomplete examples instead of discrete definitions. Does this mean that citizens were low-information voters? Many elites and wonks think so. But probably not.

In 1991, Sam Popkin coined the term 'low information signaling' in his book *Reasoning Voter*. Over the last decade, the phrase transformed to 'low information voter.' In 2016, many in the press used low-information voter to apply to Trump voters because a big percentage of his support came from voters without a college education, as though persons without a college education are automatically flipped into the pool of people who did not have enough information to make a sound vote. Are these voters low-information citizens despite their level of education or because of it? They were! *But we all are.* During an election that was supposedly about Socialism versus Capitalism, not a nickel was spent to instruct the voter about the meaning of either word nor the value or the capability or disability of either approach. Low information voter? Hardly. Low-information campaigns? Low-information political parties? High inuendo media, high anger crusades lacking information? Exactly. According to an October 2020 Virginia Commonwealth University poll, half of Biden voters were cast as votes against Trump. Likewise, 20 percent of voters were against Biden. Are low-information marketing campaigns winning elections? It would appear so.

What's the voter to think? Is the voter given enough political education to think sensibly and rationally? Not at all.

Here's the challenge. We are all low-information voters despite big media budgets for campaign marketing because by election day we are no smarter about the strategies for either party or what the most important issues are other than those issues that *test well in focus groups!* In fact, political advertising drives down our IQ. We are dumber not smarter. Whether one party leans Socialist and the other Capitalist, we have no information about how one style of governance may work better than the other. We are left in the dark and have only our anger with which to cast our votes.

Since it is not likely that electioneering will ever amount to more than propaganda, I gladly take up the challenge to convey the differences between these two ideologies. What do these terms mean? Which works? Which does not? How does each approach affect our competition with China and how should a twenty-first century government operate to improve our chances of retaining our position as leader of the free world?

Socialism versus Communism

Is there a difference?

Were Karl Marx alive to express the differences between the two, his answer would likely be *no,* the meanings are equivalent. He considered himself a Socialist and believed because man was alienated from his labor that the workers of the world would soon fall under the spell of Socialism and convert from Capitalism post haste. That did not happen.

Like most intellectual entrepreneurs Marx was not liked by the people in power—not in government, nor commerce, nor much by any institution, including a of couple of employers for which he worked, and they let him go. Without the support of Friedrich Engels, a wealthy English businessman, we may have never heard of Marx. His philosophy did not infect the masses in his home country of Germany, nor France, nor England where he published the *Communist Manifesto* and *Das Capital.* Socialism finally gained purchase in tzarist Russia where a revolution was already brewing. *The Communist Manifesto* and its dictatorship of the proletariat were a perfect fit for Leon Trotsky and Vladimir Lenin's political plans. In 1922, three years after the Revolution, the new nation was named the Union of Soviet Socialist Republics. Socialist republics, not Communist republics.

Since the Bolshevik Revolution, many nations adopted the Dictatorship of the Proletariat including Red China, Cambodia, Vietnam, North Korea, and Cuba. Communist/Socialist thinking, though, also seeped into Western nations in the 1920s and 1930s, mostly at universities. When America's political class and academia trudged to the USSR in the '20s to view this new social experiment, many received Soviet propaganda with relish. They returned to the U.S. wishing to inject these new ideas into America's political mainstream. The tragic effects of the Depression accelerated the infusion because much had been attempted to undo the economic catastrophe and good answers had been hard to come by.

The introduction of Socialism, as a brand, into a Capitalist nation was a hard lift. Americans did not much like the Socialist label. In the late 1890s the neologism for Socialism was rebranded as Progressivism, a softer, comforting naming for government with a larger footprint on American life. This naming did not work much better than Socialism; the Progressive brand became an undercurrent versus a popular movement. Over the last two elections, the use of *Progressive* versus *Socialist* vastly increased. Today, media and politicians alike attempt to soften Progressive politics, promoting the proper noun pro-gressive, without the capital P, meaning to get incrementally better. When Progressivism found little purchase in the 1930s, Franklin Roosevelt then named the Socialist approach, *liberal.* Though liberalism is about individual rights and Socialism about the state owning the individual's rights, the two definitions being totally divergent, the liberal name amazingly stuck and lib-eral is still used for the Socialist or leftist approach. Good marketing always trumps reality. In the lexicon of politics, this is a win on a grand scale.

Socialism

Traveling from Marx to the present, the meaning of Socialism has sprout-ed all categories of naming conventions and numerous styles of govern-ment: national Socialism, scientific Socialism, egalitarianism, Democratic Socialism, Progressivism, technocracy, statism, and strong central govern-ment. Marx would likely see these names to be impure, not the real stuff of Socialism. These employ a Socialist approach, a government that solves prob-lems by creating a social monopoly with strong central control but are not fully Socialist like the USSR. The Socialist approach creates one government monopoly at a time and is employed politically by almost every nation in the world. Adding political incrementalism to the Socialist approach, a land and expand strategy has worked exceptionally well for the Socialist approach and the expansion leads to a stronger and stronger central government. There is at least one commonality for all forms of Socialism; the government either owns the means of production for some set of social monopolies or selected indus-tries are so highly regulated that competition is not possible. The outcome is government-supported corporatism for a monopoly, duopoly, or oligopoly in which an open and free market ceases to exist.

Democratic Socialism, Socialism for which the citizen votes, plays well if only because candidates promote programs that give benefits to citizens to encourage their vote, for example free college, free health care, and tax credits for electric cars. If the proposition for government to a market or markets sounds good to the voter, a mix of Capitalism (open markets) and Socialism (closed markets) is erected. Nations that have voted some level of Socialism in their Capitalist markets include all of Europe, India, Australia, Canada, Japan, South Korea, the United States, and others. The United States? Really? If this is news to you, consider the previous statement, marketing trumps reality. Our education system is run via constitutional mandates in each state—which controls all means of education production—buildings, employees, payroll, etc. The same is true for our retirement system and much of our health care system.

Second and third world nations occasionally engage in revolutionary Socialism with a slightly softer spin than militant Bolshevism. Though a Socialist revolution is occasionally executed by force, modern revolutions are more about 'one vote, one time.' In this political wheelhouse, the revolutionary leader is voted into office and then changes the Constitution in ways that allow for the leader to be ruler for life: i.e., one vote once. The most visible, current example is Venezuela. Hugo Chavez took the helm at the beginning of this century and changed the constitution to end term limits. Nicolas Maduro took over when Chavez died of cancer in 2013, and despite losing an election in 2018 to Juan Guaidó, wields military power to retain his position. Nations like Venezuela are Socialist in intent, but thugocracies in execution.

Scientific Socialism creeps into the thinking of most every Socialist revolution or Socialist approach in western democracies. The theory promotes a perfect society that is designed by a special set of experts and managed by a special group of leaders. Like physics has equations that describe celestial mechanics, society, too, can aspire to the same scientific superstructure. During the COVID pandemic, "I am following the science" was a common refrain among politicians. Everyone loves to promote science as their friend, but few have much knowledge about science or its process of discovery. As well engineered as scientific Socialism sounds, the experts seldom agree about the 'science' of society, much less the science of sociology, political science, economics, or a host of other soft sciences. More on this topic later under Experts and Evolution.

Capitalism

The simplest definition of Capitalism is the matching of capital with ideas. Capital has many forms. It is very often sweat equity and savings provided by the owner of a newly formed business. Other sources of capital include monies from family, friends, vendors, banks, private investment firms, venture Capitalists, and the stock market. The value of any investment and the payback is based on the risk associated with the business venture and the ability of the business to execute and build a scalable community of consumers.

Any nation that is doing well economically has a Capitalist backbone and is a Democracy with the right to vote, generally via a multi-party system. To support Capitalist ventures, a variety of economic freedoms are required for businesses, small or large, to prosper: property rights, banking, trade, among many. Several nonprofit organizations have produced a rating system for economic freedom and rate the nations of the world. Though the United States has been a bastion of economic freedom over the last century, it has dropped down the leader board over the last decades. The greater the economic freedom, the higher the likelihood of economic success for a nation.

Like Socialism which produces a spectrum of flavors, Capitalism is not a single philosophy. There is crony Capitalism, state Capitalism, corporatism, and a Capitalist approach to government that executes via free trade, open markets, and economic freedom.

Whereas pure Socialism has been tested in several Communist dictatorships, pure Capitalism does not exist. The closest example is pre-communist Hong Kong prior to the Chinese takeover in 1999. Hong Kongers routinely enjoyed the greatest economic freedom in the world and one of the highest standards of living. Sadly, during Xi Jinping's current reign in Beijing, both political and economic freedoms in Hong Kong are under Communist attack. During 2020, the Chinese government put the city completely under its Communist thumb with a series of new security laws and the arrest of many of Hong Kong's freedom protestors. Sadly, Hong Kong has been removed by many of the nonprofits who rated each nation's economic freedom because Hong Kong is no longer considered an independent economic entity.

Both Socialism and Capitalism share common discussion points—property, state and private monopoly, and profits. Each word, though, has fully divergent tactics for Socialist or Capitalist approaches. The table of contents of this book is a menu of these sub-dialogues and each chapter will illuminate how each produce either a benefit or liability for citizens.

A final note, with an explanation point! Government is a Socialist endeavor. It owns the means to production for courts, law making, policing (FBI), printing money, the military, among many items listed in the constitution. No nation would outsource these responsibilities. The founding fathers purposely created a limited number of responsibilities to assure the power of the government would not grow so great as to diminish the liberty of its citizens. The founders understand that government, like any institution, consumes power. As power corrupts, and absolute power corrupts absolutely, so limiting government's landscape is essential to good government. In the last ninety years, the government's footprint has accelerated quickly adding many social monopolies and administrative overseers to its set of responsibilities. The final chapters of this book will examine how to better manage aging social policy that has not met the intended objectives.

PROPERTY

*"A man has a property in his opinions and
the free communication of them."*
James Madison

*"The theory of Communism may be summed up
in one sentence: Abolish all private property."*
Karl Marx

AS PROPERTY IS THE CORNERSTONE of Capitalism, it is kryptonite to Socialism. Property is the central element of the debate between the two philosophies and the history is long.

For millennia, kings, queens, tyrants, and religious leaders owned all the land and all the wealth. Their wealth depended directly on the amount of land and gold accumulated whether by war, marriage, and/or trade. Simple math. These methods of wealth creation persisted from the beginning of history until the Reformation and Renaissance when commoners began to create businesses that in turn increased trade throughout Europe and around the world. Though wealth began to accumulate for the commoner during the Renaissance, land ownership by nobility in Europe still approached 90 percent. Farmers rented land from the nobility and paid dearly for the privilege to plant and harvest. In cities, rents were collected by the king's men or the church for their properties which included domiciles and businesses. Commoners entered the ownership mix and because of their growing wealth, individual property rights evolved.

In 1690, John Locke wrote the *Second Treatise of Government* and reset the very core of western civilization's view of man and property. For Locke, property is an essential right of nature, a key component of Locke's theory about mankind's freedoms. He named three natural rights: life, liberty, and estate. He writes:

> Sect. 87. Man being born, as has been proved, with a title to perfect free-dom, and an uncontrouled enjoyment of all the rights and privileges of the law of nature, equally with any other man, or number of men in the world, hath by nature a power, not only to preserve his property, that is,

his life, liberty and estate, against the injuries and attempts of other men; but to judge of, and punish the breaches of that law in others, as he is persuaded the offence deserves, even with death itself, in crimes where the heinousness of the fact, in his opinion, requires it. (Locke, Second Treatise of Government, 1690)

Locke's notion of estate included not just land as we might commonly think today but also our bodies and our labor. Over the last 330 years, the definition of property has expanded to include our homes and the contents, stocks, bonds, the dollars in our savings and checking accounts, businesses and their assets, intellectual property, and patents. The land we own as a person or business includes surface rights to build a home or to farm or harvest its trees and agriculture. Land rights also include mineral rights for what lies under the surface. Without these rights, we, like commoners and serfs before them, have nothing. Literally, nothing. We are wards of the state, regardless of the nature of the government.

As the western world moved through the Renaissance into the Industrial Age, ownership of physical property transitioned from kings, queens, and popes to an evolving class of rich business owners and commoners. In America, where arable land had an inexhaustible supply, anyone could own land, with ownership requiring only the sweat equity to clear land and the employment of a surveyor to mark the property and register it with the local authorities. America was an economic game changer for the world because of its wealth of 'free' land available to everyone. Labor coupled with land in an agricultural economy translated to growing wealth.

Though the king owned most of Great Britain and mountains of gold and jewels, along with extensive powers and prerogatives, John Locke proposed that kings had no special leadership rights, no divine right of kings, no special Godly gifts. With simple logic, he proposed that if we all descended from Adam, and Adam had no special right to leadership and had to count on God for his existence, then kings did not enjoy divine rights to leadership, and thus led only by power and force, not from God's divination of corporal power. Conversely, if Adam enjoyed divine right, then so must we all.

All these premises having, as I think, been clearly made out, it is impossible that the rulers now on earth should make any benefit, or derive any the least shadow of authority from that, which is held to be the fountain of all power, Adam's private dominion and paternal jurisdiction; so that he that will not give just occasion to think that all government in the world is the product only of force and violence, and that men live together by no other rules but that of beasts, where the strongest carries it, and so lay a foundation for perpetual disorder.

The intersection of the natural rights of man with evolving property rights coupled with the dubious thinking about the Divine Right of Kings and their near monopoly of land ownership provided great intellectual support for the rising political position of commoners. In England, Europe, and the Colonies commoners had more say about who leads and who should have the ability to own land. The ability for all to own property (and not just land, but ideas, labor, etc.) paralleled the improvement of law with the precise definition of land including its location and dimensions as well as any structures. In America, the surveyor became an increasing important job as anyone could claim land with the surveyor's professional assistance.

The First Socialist—then Marx

Less than one hundred years after Locke's *Second Treatise*, across the English Channel in France, Jean Jacques Rousseau took an alternate view of property in *A Discourse on Inequality*. He lamented the inequality created by property being held by so few. For those who believe the constant thrum of income inequality is a twentieth century news item, Rousseau wrote his book in 1754. At the center of the inequality problem lay property, of which the nobility and church owned nearly all. His thoughts on the nature of property:

The first man who, having enclosed a piece of ground, to whom it occurred to say this is mine, and found people sufficiently simple to believe him, was the true founder of civil society. How many crimes, wars, murders, how many miseries and horrors Mankind would have been spared by him who, pulling up the stakes or filling in the ditch, had cried out to his kind: Beware of listening to this impostor; You are lost if you forget that the fruits are everyone's and the Earth no-one's. (Rousseau, Discourse of Inequality)

Rousseau did not have a ready answer to the dilemma of land ownership nor the conflicts it inevitably created, but it is easy to see how Marx picked up on this theme a half century later.

Though Marx's Socialist philosophy centered on man's alienation from his labor, property was his highest priority in optimizing society for mankind's benefit. In *The Communist Manifesto*, Marx lists the top priorities for engineering a perfect Socialist society. The Dictatorship of the Proletariat lays out ten objectives:

- Abolition of property in land and application of all rents of land to public purposes.
- A heavy progressive or graduated income tax.
- Abolition of all right of inheritance.
- Confiscation of the property of all emigrants and rebels.
- Centralisation of credit in the hands of the State, by means of a national bank with State capital and an exclusive monopoly.
- Centralisation of the means of communication and transport in the hands of the State.
- Extension of factories and instruments of production owned by the State; the bringing into cultivation of waste-lands, and the improvement of the soil generally in accordance with a common plan.
- Equal liability of all to labour. Establishment of industrial armies, especially for agriculture.
- Combination of agriculture with manufacturing industries; gradual abolition of the distinction between town and country, by a more equable distribution of the population over the country.
- Free education for all children in public schools. Abolition of children's factory labour in its present form. Combination of education with industrial production, &c., &c. (Marx, Karl; Engels, Friedrich. *The Communist Manifesto* (p. 22). Public Domain Books. Kindle Edition.)

Although this book will not directly discuss the other nine bullets for Marx's engineering of a perfect society, the abolition of property is a cornerstone of Marx's thinking. He understood that without property rights, Capitalism ceased to exist, so its abolition was essential to Socialist philosophy. Corollary to the property ownership problem were the huge rents that kings, queens, and popes collected from the commoners (and serfs) that rented property from the nobility. For Marx, this aging collective run by the king would be replaced with rents now going to the Dictator of the Proletariat. Marx changed property ownership from one dictator to another, but also ended the chance for the common man to own any type of property, including his own body, his labor or a business.

If the other nine bullets have a familiar ring emanating from one or both parties in Washington during election cycles, they should because the ring is loud and true. Should the reader be concerned that so many of today's political objectives echo Marx's objectives? I will let the reader decide.

From Socialism to the Socialist Approach

How have property rights evolved since the Russian Revolution until today? Legislators around the world have been busy. The most serious challenge to property ownership is regulation. Some regulation is good and needed, and some is regulation meant to create barriers to ownership. From a Socialist perspective, the modern trend is *if you cannot get rid of a supposed problem, regulate it out of existence,* including property. This takes shape as legislation, federal programs, executive orders, and the expansion of the administrative state's regulatory structure created outside of the halls of Congress. A recent example: Land rights have been mitigated with respect to environment policy and regulation. Clear air and water and the regulations to assure their cleanliness are great, but sometimes politicians go beyond safety.

During the 2016 campaign, Hilary Clinton stated, *"We're going to put a lot of coal miners and coal companies out of business."* Regarding execution of putting an industry out of business, Congress never passed a law making coal prohibitively expensive, but the administrative state did take up the cause with new carbon dioxide rules that treated CO_2 as a pollutant. As new regulations increased the cost of coal during the Obama Administration, these rules were relaxed under the Trump administration. While rules came and went depending on which party was in charge, market innovations transformed energy, with huge new American supplies of inexpensive natural gas via fracking. More than anti-coal regulations, cheap natural gas reduced the coal footprint in America extending a thousand-year trend for less expensive, cleaner fuel. Flipping back to additional government interference, construction permits for gas and oil pipelines have been stopped during this century, stopped, started, and stopped again by legal challenges. As Joe Biden came to office, his stated campaign promise to stop the construction of the Keystone Pipeline, came to fruition with an executive order on his first day. The pipeline actually reduces CO2 as trucks are not needed to move fuel. When politics overplay sensibility, problems are not solved but exacerbated.

In western Capitalist democracies with Socialist underpinnings, the incremental expansion of social monopolies is the cost of legislative negotiation which trades commercial and military initiatives for additional increases in social welfare. Incrementalism also arrives via the administrative state and executive orders, adding burdensome and expensive rules to achieve goals that cannot be achieved in the legislative branch. Worse for Americans, the constant oscillation between the two ideologies makes consistent and wise investment in energy, anti-poverty, education—or anything—a bit of a poop shoot, which is a costly drag on our economy. The Competitive Enterprise Institute estimates the cost of government regulations to be just under $2 trillion dollars or about 10 percent of GDP. Our regulatory environment is so complex that it is not unlike the barrier to property ownership in the third world. As the regulatory environment is extended by Democrats, then reduced by Republicans, businesses become reluctant investors as whatever rules currently apply will likely change every two, four or eight years.

The bad habits of cronyism extend well beyond the west industrialized nations. The administrative law approach is exploited in the world's poorest nations where the rich own most of the land and do not wish to part with their treasure. This is the worst kind of corporatism to reduce the freedoms of the poor. Hernando de Soto's brilliant book *The Mystery of Capital* highlights the litany of legal complexities involving land ownership around the world, especially in third world and former Communist nations that inhibit the free exchange and ownership of property. Mr. de Soto estimates the complexity of property laws that create barriers to ownership translates into nearly $9 trillion in extralegal property which cannot be leveraged as equity for new capital. If these nations streamlined rules for property ownership and increased transparency of purchase/sell transactions, de Soto estimates that global GDP growth in these countries could grow as high as 10 percent annually.

Property rights are essential to economic success. In many countries, the complexity of property law protects the landed to the exclusion of the landless who have lived on 'extra-legal' land for decades but are nevertheless title-less. Citizens simply squat on property in lieu of attempting to endure the hardship of legally acquiring the land which takes years and tens to hundreds of legal steps. These arduous legal steps help lawyers protect the landed but assure that free and reasonable exchange of title for new ownership is all but impossible. Per de Soto:

> In Haiti, one way an ordinary citizen can settle legally on government land is first to lease it from the government for five years and then buy it. Working with associates in Haiti, our researchers found that to obtain such a least took 65 bureaucratic steps – requiring, on average, a little more than two years – all for the privilege of merely leasing the land for five years. To buy the land required another 111 bureaucratic hurdles – and twelve more years. Total time to gain lawful land in Haiti: nineteen years. ... In fact, in every country we investigated, we found that it is very nearly as difficult to stay legal as it is to become legal.' (Soto, The Mystery of Capital, 2000, p. 4)

The Haiti example may seem more like Capitalist overloads protecting their treasures, and this is correct, but the same tactic is executed by Socialists for other types of property, especially business concerns. In this case, Socialists and Capitalists use the same tools to keep the masses at bay. Marx believed that Socialism was a replacement for Capitalism. The result, though, has been to replace kings, queens and popes with Socialism's elites, experts and secular theists. One tyranny replaces another.

In America, with property as the central economic success variable, both rich Capitalists and wealthy Socialists are using political tools, via regulation and law, to depreciate the common man's access to property. Corporatists of both creeds cozy up to legislators via lobbyists hoping to protect the status quo. Though the Socialists have been far more effective than Capitalists in engineering their desires, there should be no doubt that both groups tend to look down their noses at the rest of us while assuring the needs of monied friends are secured.

Property, though, as Locke recommended, is and should be an essential protected freedom. "Government has no other end, but the preservation of property." Considering that our basic property rights include our bodies, our labor and our ideas, his proposition is crucial to our individual success. Our economic freedom is one measure of whether we are succeeding in protecting our rights to the various forms of property. An abolition of property in Communist nations translated into a total economic failure for every Communist adventure because without property, there is no path to create new ideas, which create wealth, investment, and more ideas and then more economic growth. Our freedom to own property, including our labor, is essential to our personal, corporate, and national success. In any nation where the right to own property is abridged by law or challenged by excessively complex regulation, economic success is all but impossible.

Voters should beware of politicians touting their Socialist credentials or Socialist approach to government. Additional barriers to ownership of land and its uses will reduce economic activity in the name of good intentions but have all too often produced poor results. Alternatively, voters should also beware of Capitalist politicians working with lobbyists whose only job is to protect the wealth of rich clients whether they be businesses, foundations, unions, or special interests.

Do today's Socialists tout the same end to private property promoted by Marx? Some perhaps, but mostly they do not. Their heavy political hand and incremental approach to creeping Socialism though, has hung an anchor on many a commoner via restrictive association laws, regulation promoting rent control, high real estate taxes, and excessive federal intrusions that run from taxation to land use rights, to burdensome regulation, and poorly performing, and expensive, social monopolies.

Cronyism: From Socialism to Capitalism, and Back

Crony Capitalism is an oblique approach to Socialism that uses the administrative and legislative state to protect business friends, usually big businesses. Government, big business, and lobbyists work together to provide rules to reduce their tax burden or protect their competitive position. For example, according to a 2010 *New York Times* article, by Pat Cohen,

258 "profitable Fortune 500 companies" paid no taxes because of numerous tax loopholes. Tax credits are used to produce benefits for rich corporations. General Electric, among many manufacturers, worked with Congress to create energy tax credits for appliances. We all want to save energy, right? What could go wrong? Only 30 percent of taxpayers had access to these credits as only 30 percent itemize deductions for their federal taxes. The other 70 percent that do not itemize do not get these tax benefits. The energy tax credit increased sales of appliances which increases the profitability for appliance makers. Would GE have built appliances that were increasingly energy efficient anyway? Of course, they would because energy efficiency is what consumers prefer. Those that benefited from the credit, however, were the wealthy and GE, not the regular folks, the commoner.

The same kind of crony thinking is used via a Socialist approach to sell electric cars and solar panels. As these products are expensive, they are affordable only to the richest consumers. Does making electric cars more affordable to the rich seem reasonable? It does not. The challenge for the average Joe who would love an electric car is that even with tax credits, the electric car is unaffordable. To make matters worse, the 90 percent of consumers that are *not* rich enough to afford an electric car are paying federal taxes to fund credits for rich people to buy electric cars that they could afford *without* the tax credit. If making the rich richer is the goal, then this makes sense. The tax credits also create irrational exuberance in the stock market. Tesla's total stock value outpaced the nine largest automakers: Volkswagen, Toyota, Nissan, Hyundai, GM, Ford, Honda, Fiat Chrysler, and Peugeot despite sales that are only a tiny fraction of the total sales of these manufacturers making Elon Musk one of the richest men in the world. The rich are getting richer with government help. Is this good government policy considering that even if every car in America were electric, the reduction of greenhouse gases would not top 5 percent? Is this the best policy for reducing CO_2. Probably not. This is crony Socialism at its worst. Crony Socialists mimicking crony Capitalists should leave a bitter taste in the voter's mouth. The rich get richer with sponsorship from our dear friends in Washington. Crony Socialist and Capitalist approaches to central industrial planning is good neither for the poor nor the middle class, and worse—regarding climate—the reduction of carbon dioxide in the air from electric cars is miniscule. But rich Capitalists and wealthy Socialists alike are winners. Average Joes, not so much.

The Plymouth Company: 1606

In 1606, King James and a small group of knights, wealthy business-men and owners of English agricultural estates established The Plymouth Company, a joint-stock company. The company's purpose was to fund settlements along America's eastern seaboard. The dollars that purchased the stock financed the settler's trip in return for repayment of expenses from the profits of the colony. This first step toward Capitalism is remarkably interesting in that England was still steeped in mercantilist economics.

The colony was set up as a common store and for what was produced, each colonist got one share. This communal, i.e., Socialist, tactic during the first year of operation did not work well. Everyone got an equal share regardless of the amount of work done reducing the motivation for hard work by some and causing hard feelings for many. The productivity of the commune plummeted. William Bradford, the colony's leader, noted in his journal: "For this community was found to breed much confusion and discontent, and retard much employment that would have been to their benefit and comfort…" No one owned the land they worked nor the value of their labor, it being homogenized into the common store. Seeing that the originally contracted approach was not working, Bradford assigned each family a plot of land to work. Bradford: "This had very good success for it made all hands industrious." Industriousness is not only a measure of our value but also a key variable in happiness.

Plymouth employed elements of corporatism. The king and his buddies formed a private stock company to collectively own land in a geography to which they had no legal right. The king enjoyed legislative, executive, and judicial prerogatives that empowered his ability to form a business to enrich his friends and himself. He did not need the lobbyists that today's corporatists use because the king held all the power to execute his will, the will of the State.

Most important, though, Bradford was the type of leader that when the collective approach did not work, he did not double down as most modern politicians do. He changed. He adapted. He allowed the solution to evolve.

Flexibility is essential to great leadership. It is also essential to the success of modern government, something we are sorely lacking. Providing individual property rights spurred personal industry, which increased crop yields which produced profits for the stock company, which encouraged more investment in America. Colonialism is not the best of breed governance, but the investment in the Bay Colony caused a flood of industrious commoners to migrate to America. Their progey would fight the ultimate fight for freedom in 1776.

The Mortgage/Financial Crisis of 2009

Moving ahead 400 years, regulation, and policy to help the poorest can also have the direst impact. Good intentions are never enough to produce good results and without common sense and foresight even good intentions can be dangerous.

The law of unintended consequences ruled the crash of 2009. Often our federal leaders attempt to orchestrate good intentions via legislative effort. Home ownership is an important economic indicator. The more of us who own a home, the more personal wealth is increased. Owning a home improves our monthly finances, if only to lock in the cost of mortgage over long periods of time, and with a mortgage payoff, that last payment guarantees reduced expenses during retirement. For the poor, home ownership can be the ticket out of poverty. Home equity can provide an economic bridge in tough times, without which the poor—The Forgotten Man—suffer greatly.

For low-income earners, qualifying for home loans is a huge challenge. Numerous federal programs have attempted to increase home ownership including the Community Reinvestment Act and federal home loan programs like FHA, the Federal Housing Authority. The Community Reinvestment Act ended redlining in poor neighborhoods. Even the federal insurance programs Fannie Mae (Federal National Mortgage Association) and Freddie Mac (Federal Home Loan Mortgage Corporation) have assisted home purchases by the financially challenged by buying, insuring, and packaging non-qualified mortgages from commercial mortgage businesses.

In the late 1990s, to further aid low-income earners, the federal government relaxed loan qualification standards allowing 'no-docs' qualification and 'stated income' loan applications. A buyer could buy a home without income documentation and could simply state their income as evidence of their ability to pay. What could go wrong with this relaxation in an industry—banking—known to be the greediest of industries? Everything. Wrapping these new qualification features into protection of poorly qualified but government guaranteed loans accelerated purchases and prices for homes skyrocketed.

Under the watchful eye of Congress and the Federal Reserve, interest rates dropped to under 5 percent in the early 2000s. Mortgage originators created numerous new mortgage tools to hype home purchases: ARMs (Adjustable-rate mortgage) were popularized. Balloon payment home purchases, generally a gamble that only rich, sophisticated buyers employed, increased in popularity. A buyer could originate a mortgage for 1 percent interest for five years; then the rate increased to the market interest rate, meaning the monthly payment jumped, too. No-down mortgages were allowed. Even mortgages with a negative down payment were allowed. Congress and the administrative agencies reduced loan qualification rules so that 'stated income' and no-docs mortgages became routine.

The market raced, especially for lower income home buyers who took advantage of relaxed qualification.

Freddie and Fannie had billions of dollars in questionable loans packaged into mortgage-backed securities, a bundle of hundreds or thousands of mortgages which were peddled as all Class A paper. The home market peaked and began to sag, and when homeowners' ARMs jumped to higher interest rates that poor owners could not pay, and when those owners could not sell in a market that was slipping, the lack of transparency of these failing mortgage bundles were the tip of the spear for the financial market which collapsed.

Was the problem caused by greedy Capitalists? Absolutely.

Did the government's relaxation of qualification rules create more greed? Undeniably.

Did the government encourage mortgage lenders to lend more and more, regardless of qualification of the potential homeowner to pay the mortgage? Utterly.

You can blame the business community, but they were doing exactly what the government suggested and for that the government is fully responsible for the collapse. They created a bubble which relied on bundles of mortgages whose variance in value, mortgage by mortgage, was invisible to the investor. Differing mortgages were treated like a share of Apple stock, all having equal value. Looking back, this is completely nuts. The unintended consequences of good intentions without good sense is a common theme in both parties' leadership.

For all the blame that mortgage companies and banks deserve, our leaders are ultimately culpable. Their first responsibility is to *plan for the competition,* not to lay out an organized strategy for greed. Hayek recommended planning as, ". . . planning and competition can be combined only by planning for competition but not by planning against competition." Capitalism is at its worst when the government takes its eyes off their responsibility for simple, thoughtful regulation, especially when it diminishes the ability of businesses to compete and votes to favor one competing product against another.

The road to hell is paved with good intentions, especially when the rules for competition defy common sense. That anyone . . . *anyone* . . . would deign to believe that relieving markets of basic qualification rules for mortgages is a good idea is hard to fathom. There were no calls by our 537 elected officials nor any executive branch leaders that called out 'no docs' or 'stated income' standards as being problematic.

Smoothing the road from burdensome regulation to simple, smart, and effective regulation is no easy task, but Capitalism is only as good and wise as the government which makes the rules for the competition. Socialism assumes that our leaders know how to design a high-functioning, efficient and effective regulatory regime, a controlling approach that has proven to be more about government control than smart regulation. Both approaches, especially where political parties collude, are responsible. Interestingly, the finger-pointing by both sides was directed outside Washington. No one took responsibility for creating the greed in the mortgage market. The result was the 20,000-page Dodd-Frank Wall Street Reform and Consumer Protection Act of 2010. It featured utter complexity in response to a simple problem for loan qualification.

Conclusion

Without private ownership of property, creating wealth is impossible. Property has a broad meaning beyond land: plant and equipment, homes, cars and trucks, stock and bonds, savings, profits and most important for this century—ideas. Ideas are essential for the creation of wealth. Collections of wealth from individuals and businesses are invested to create more wealth, more jobs, more innovations, and more ideas. When property is abolished or its use mitigated, wealth is absorbed by the state via taxes, or in the case of many Socialist states by government acquisition. In western nations, the state has a terrible track record of producing positive results from its allocation of your income/wealth for new state-sponsored endeavors, whether social monopolies or tax preferences for favored industries.

The inability of the state to allocate its resources effectively is precisely why the USSR and Red China failed. Their leaders invested poorly. State factories rotted. The environment went to hell. In 2010, on a business trip to China to promote products to clean the air in waste plants and factories, one government leader (who also ran the plant) suggested to me that the government had other priorities above the need of clean air. Because no one owned the plant, no one was responsible for either clean air or the plant's upkeep. Profits went to the local government authority and were spent for who knows what.

The Socialists in America are not out to take your land or home, but the constraints proposed by leftist or conservative cronyist leaders should be concerning and raise a red flag for your vote. Americans should be wary of any politician—Socialist or Capitalist, Republican or Democrat—that is too cozy with big Capitalists or big unionists and their lobbyists. These relationships are about protecting the treasure of big money, not the rights of the individual, and these relationships are dangerous to the economic success of our nation and the roots of our Democracy.

Our economic freedoms encompassing property rights are essential for our economic success, personally, corporately, and nationally. Without property, all other freedoms wither, economies slow, and the magnet to attract the world's best and brightest is diminished.

If there is a single variable that should promote a Capitalist versus a Socialist approach, it is the freedom to own property. The challenges of property ownership, as Rousseau noted, create dustups from time to time, but the dustups are far outweighed by its ability to create value, income, wealth, and support for new ideas which are the central variable of twenty-first century economic success.

IDEAS

"The test of a first-rate intelligence is the ability to hold two opposed ideas in mind at the same time and still retain the ability to function."
F. Scott Fitzgerald

"Ideas are the currency of twenty-first century economic success."
Tom Lewellen

OF COURSE, NEW IDEAS HAVE always been front and center to moving the economic ball forward. Today, the pace of new ideas has accelerated fantastically.

The nation producing the most new ideas, especially disruptive ideas, will top the global economic ladder. For the last one hundred years, America has been both the idea engine and the economic catalyst for the world. This century, China has edged into the lead for creating new and expanding businesses, albeit their production is heavily lifted by the theft of western ideas. But even theft of ideas, an element of Capitalism, is essential to fuel their economic missile, and that Capitalist missile is pointed directly at America and western democracies.

Schumpeter considered that combining Socialism and Capitalism would be a heavy lift. It turns out this has not been the case. Not only have western Capitalist nations adopted a Socialist approach by building social monopolies into a Capitalist superstructure, at least two Communist nations, China, and Vietnam, have inserted a dollop of Capitalism into their dictatorships producing great economic success. Their Capitalist experiments are working and working quite well. What did they do? They injected limited property rights into their Socialist constitutions.

As earlier noted in Marx's ten to-dos for the Dictatorship of the Proletariat, property rights are a Communist no-no, if only because Marx understood that property rights were the foundation of Capitalism, the ideology he aimed to replace.

Why would China, the world's preeminent Communist nation, include property as a right when Marx had emphasized that the abolition of property was a Communist prerequisite? As much as anything, for 5,000 years, China's cultural conceit was that they should be at the top of the world's social, cultural, military, and economic ladder. Communism, though, did not have the economic tools to grow the economy. Without a little Capitalism, China would wind up on the historical and economic ash heap like the USSR. The USSR ran out of money trying to compete with the U.S. militarily and did an economic belly flop in 1989. Without some modest level of individual property rights, creating wealth was severely hampered if not completely obviated. To assure they could compete with the U.S., China decided a little Capitalism was not a bad thing.

China's cultural vanity is complemented by the belief that the rest of the world is inhabited by barbarians. Beyond this vanity, especially over the last 700 years, history showed a hugely different leaderboard. The modern barbarians from the Reformation to today's western industrialized nations have been at the top of the social, cultural, military, and economic hierarchy, putting China in their place more than a few times, sometimes with great humiliation to their leaders and populace.

In the twentieth century, Mao's Cultural Revolution and *The Little Red Book* left China penniless and an international pariah. Fifteen years after Mao's death in 1976, with some modest economic reforms, the poverty rate still exceeded 90 percent with more than a billion people living on less the $5.50 a day. Over the course of the next thirty years, however, Chinese strategy changed. With an infusion of Capitalist tools, including new individual property rights, banking reforms and induction into the World Trade Organization, the poverty rate dropped to 25 percent, lifting 600,000,000 citizens into the middle class. Their Capitalist success put them at number two on the world's GDP competition, not far behind the United States and with economic growth that will allow the Chinese to surpass the United States and move to number one by 2030.

The new Chinese motto could have been, *if you can't beat them, join them*. China's success sprung from an insight from Deng Xiaoping in 1978, a few years after the death of Mao Zedong. Deng recommends:

To make revolution and build socialism we need large numbers of path breakers who dare to think, explore new ways and generate new ideas.

Deng's statement is the key to why Capitalism creates economic growth, expanding incomes and wealth and Socialism does not. Ideas are essential to economic success. That constitutional edits now allowed ownership of property—including ideas—transformed a dead economy into a dynamic idea engine.

Under Mao, all ideas were owned by Mao. There was no possibility for a citizen to own an idea that would create income or wealth. Ideas like property were only for public use. Though the members of the Red Chinese politburo probably lobbed in a few ideas, no economic benefit was received by any person. All benefit went to Mao, the State, and the Party.

Deng was not the first Communist to notice that Communist economies had low or no potential for growth, though he was the first to do something about the problem by rethinking property rights. He understood that the reason for laggard growth lay squarely upon the inability to encourage new ideas from their prodigious citizenry. Why would any citizen wish to create an idea that provided no personal benefit? Considering that ideas are a type of property, changing the constitution to allow for property rights was an incredible game changer. If anyone could own property, albeit that ownership was suborned to the State, then ideas could proliferate, and they did. Over the last thirty years, economic growth has averaged nearly 10 percent with a million new businesses a year and as many new patents. Whereas the Red Chinese idea factory employed only a single person, Mao, today, all 1.4 billion Chinese citizens can join Deng's idea creation revolution.

Though new ideas and innovation have always been important to economic success, this century, as innovation in technology and life sciences accelerate, ideas are *the* coinage of economic achievement. The more new ideas, especially creatively destructive ideas described by Schumpeter, the greater the probability of that nation's economic, social, and cultural success. New ideas and the new businesses they precipitate provide a supply of tomorrow's new members to the Fortune 500. A steady and large stream of new ideas are the funnel for our future demand-side economy.

Does Chinese Socialism work, even when a light touch of economic freedom for generating new ideas is added to its otherwise totalitarian mix? The answer is Yes! Schumpeter may have been surprised by the mix of Socialism and Capitalism. American leaders, though, should pay attention because the converse provides insight as well. Increasing Socialist administration of government reduces economic freedom and diminishes growth because government limits ideas when increasing regulation and the expanse of government footprint of responsibilities. While many of the Left have admitted their admiration of Chinese central and industrial planning as a good model, they have missed the fact that these Socialist economic levers wielded by any government diminish, not enhance, the growth produced by amplified freedoms for property, capital investment, and free trade.

With only a lean superstructure for property rights, the resultant increase in ideas Deng sought has helped produce great Chinese economic growth. Though over the next decade Chinese economic growth will slow to around 6 percent from 10 percent, the Chinese economy will eclipse America's. While China experiments with increasing economic freedoms, America is moving in the other direction. Our government is poorly run and spending wildly grandly with poor financial and social results. Our social monopolies perform inadequately while the government grows and costs spiral. Without an economic game plan to assure faster growth, our children may not live the great lives we hope as China will be able to extend its heavy fingers into our economic pie.

Economist William Easterly, in the *Tyranny of Experts*, wrote that the generation of ideas by any nation is proportional to its population. This makes sense. More people produce more ideas. Additionally, the freer citizens are to have an idea as well as the freedom to execute a plan to share that idea broadly, the more likely that idea will reach the marketplace of ideas and generate income and wealth. Without an iota of individual freedom during Mao's reign, ideas were trapped inside the heads of its citizens. The same challenge exists for any Communist nation. With expanded property freedoms, China will continue to grow allowing another 600 billion people to escape poverty over the coming decades. Conversely, America's economic freedoms flopped back and forth between two parties between two styles of government with divergent principles of governance, both increasingly depriving citizens of their economic freedom. The greatest loss of freedom: a dwindling paycheck diminished by high taxation and lost productivity associated with needlessly extensive and complex regulation.

The one-size-fits-all Socialist approach, though it may be needed rarely, is an idea diminisher, a killer of innovation. Once the law/policy/program is implemented, it is locked in concrete by vested interests, (businesses, unions, special interest groups, all generally monied) that work diligently to keep the solution alive, ever-expanding, regardless of social or financial results. These political interests will fight to their economic death to assure the immortality of the solution and that the paradigm is never challenged. One size, one vote, forever. Even when one-size-fits-all solutions fail, instead of adjustments or renovations that would improve social results and/or financial stability, political interests ask for more money, usually in the form of new taxes to prop up failing systems. Not only is the possibility of new ideas destroyed, but the Socialist approach becomes more and more financially unsustainable as social results stagnate or fail.

Socialism, Science and Monopolies

All Socialists purport to follow the science, so scientific Socialism at its root is just Socialism. Many utopians, like Marx, believed that the perfect society could be engineered in the same manner that scientists use the scientific method. Socialists see science through the lens of Isaac Newton who, in *Principia*, codified celestial mechanics and gravity. Most of us learned Newton's three laws of motion in high school physics. Newton proposed: Force equals Mass times Acceleration. Every object in a state of uniform motion tends to remain in that state of motion unless an external force is applied to it. And, for every action there is an equal and opposite reaction. With these three simple laws, Newton described the entire universe. Utopians thought they could apply the simplicity of physics to social sciences and design a perfect society with equal simplicity and results. Scientific Socialism, Progressivism, National Socialism, technocracy, and statism have adopted the belief that social engineering is *the* scientific process to form a perfect society. The corollary of this thinking is that there are a few, incredibly special people that have the capability to design the perfect society, culture and economy or something close to it.

Except science, even Newton's Three Laws, are not one-and-done science. Most science is about failure, not success in a single stroke. In a *Wall Street Journal* article about the COVID crisis, Matt Ridley *writes:*

In a lecture at Cornell University in 1964, the physicist Richard Feynman defined the scientific method. First, you guess, he said, to a ripple of laughter. Then you compute the consequences of your guess. Then you compare those consequences with the evidence from observations or experiments. If [your guess] disagrees with experiment, it's wrong. In that simple statement is the key to science. It does not make a difference how beautiful the guess is, how smart you are, who made the guess or what his name is...it's wrong.'

Scientist and science historian Michael Strevens, like Feynman, challenges the belief that science is a one-time, easy-to-discover, winner-take-all proposition. In his book *The Knowledge Machine*, Strevens writes that even scientists are challenged by what exactly science is and how to accomplish scientific discovery:

Carry out a poll of the scientific profession, then, and you will soon discover that although scientists know very well how to implement their methods, they don't know what it is about those methods that really matters and why. . . I believe...science is an alien thought form.

Whereas non-scientist, political figures on the Left tell us they are following the science or that they love science, most do not understand what science is. Politicians use their affinity for science as a marketing term, not an intellectual endeavor. Strevens further states that as scientists are challenged by their methods and processes, they are also co-opted by social, cultural, and political inputs. Subjectivity flavors their objectivity. He is correct and not just for those in scientific professions. The rest of us tend to shy away from math or science courses unless they are an academic requirement and then most students take the easiest possible option. Few read about science and fewer press outlets write about it because of low reader interest. Since scientific articles have limited readership, they produce less ad revenue and thus even fewer articles are published. Strevens adds, *"It seems, to all the world, that there is something about the nature of science itself that the human race finds hard to take on board."*

Beware of the political marketing around 'following the science.' Most of us, including politicians, would not be able to judge what is science and what is fiction given a lifetime of effort. The Left, and an occasional conversative, are happy to let you know they are on board *The Science Machine*, as long as it is one-size-fits-all and aligns with their ideological philosophy.

Science, it turns out, is more like an evolution of ideas or a marketplace of ideas. Science is not a one-and-done idea some genius creates in a darkened laboratory. Hypothesis, observe, test, results . . . and back to hypothesis seems to be a never-ending cycle. Newton's Three Laws held up perfectly for three hundred years until they were significantly upgraded; Einstein proposed the Theory of Relativity, which showed the universe to be curvy around very heavy objects and even more curvy when objects moved close to the speed of light. Newton's notion of celestial mechanics and gravity and his resultant flat universe were summarily transformed. Then only seventy-five years after Einstein's theory, scientists proposed that dark matter and dark energy existed. New data about spinning galaxies did not match the expected results from Newtonian or Einstein's notions of gravity. This update is still in progress.

If the Left understood science, they would know that it is very unlikely any person exists or will ever exist that could write down the precepts for erecting a perfect society, or a perfect anything, even with access to unlimited data about individuals and society. Why? Because we are constantly evolving. Humanity is nowhere near a point of history where new ideas cease to arrive and evolve. Great ideas do not come along that often, and science is only able to find grand, universal answers after arduous work and testing, and even then, the universe changes as new and better data challenges old solutions.

The challenge for business ideas is even greater. It takes about 10,000 new business formations over many years to create a single, highly successful, Fortune 500 business. Ninety percent of new businesses fail in the first year. The weeding process in business markets is not unlike the vetting process in science which assures that bad ideas do not make much of a splash and generally find their way to the ash heap. Most business ideas like scientific notions and political proposals end up in failure. What Feynman said earlier about science is also true of business and of any idea. Given the challenges of science, the voter should not expect that a small group of political representatives of high intelligence, great personal conceit, and questionable common sense can, in short order, whip up a perfectly functioning social monopoly. Although many citizens talk about term limits for politicians, term limits for policy need to be considered, at least as an exit strategy when original hypotheses fail.

Markets are much like the scientific method proposed by Francis Bacon in 1620. Thousands and thousands of scientific hypotheses are tested every year and some hypotheses are validated by the data. When a hypothesis is validated, new data accumulated with better tools will likely require new solutions. It's all about the data and methods to acquire, validate and analyze it. Markets work much the same way, except that consumers scrutinize the data, and *we* vote to validate products and services instead of having scientists test theories to validate hypotheses.

There is no one-and-done solution, not in the hard sciences, the soft sciences, in business, nor in politics and public policy. As we evolve, new ideas replace old ideas. The voter should be highly skeptical of anyone that proposes a few talented wonks in D.C. can whip up a solution for health care or education or anything that will have sustainably positive social and financial results. If Newton, Einstein, and Zwicky (dark matter) could not finally resolve the equations for gravity over five hundred years, and their collective IQ could very well be higher than that of Congress, it is not remotely possible that collaborators in Washington can do something during a two-year election cycle that will have much merit, except to get reelected by propagandizing their great effort and good intentions.

The Left has a deep belief that a few special people can create flawless, unbending policy and a program, with no flexibility for the solution's evolution, and without testing the notion (something scientists consider essential). This belief has produced an endless litany of programs that are well-intended but underperforming. Ultimately, the Socialist approach significantly abates idea formation in favor of perpetual, one-size-fits-all solutions.

That a special class of problem solvers is presumed to exist, mimics Marx's two-class society: the elites, experts and secular theists who rule and the rest of us, the commoners whose duty it is to follow their every directive. How America and other western nations injected such an ethos into a Democracy is not inexplicable. Socialism is imminently marketable. It sounds great on the campaign trail. Socialism, though, with this privileged perspective of elites and experts (including their science teammates) is precisely the kind of governance our Founders fought to discard. The tyrants and kings and popes believed in the same kind of two-class society: The elites are in power and everyone else follows obediently. Socialism, in all its flavors, is elitist. Ideas from the limited group of natural superiors at the top of the political food chain are foisted on those at the bottom. Because of their limited numbers, they produce a limited set of ideas that once legislated are set in stone, immutable and immortal, regardless of their efficacy.

The more power allotted to the elites, then, the more idea creation is diminished. Socialism is relegated to autocracy and limited imagination for new ideas. It is an idea killer.

Capitalism, Religion and Markets

Capitalism and Democracy were just getting their embryonic legs during the Industrial Revolution. The initial conditions for free enterprise began much earlier with Jesus Christ, Apostle Paul, and Martin Luther. Capitalism spawned from cultural and religious underpinnings. One key element of Luther's 95 Theses nailed to the door of the Catholic Church in Wittenberg Germany in 1463 was that by Saint Paul's directive 'faith alone' was the essential component to heaven's entry. The derivatives that followed, vast deviations from the Catholic Church's central authority in Rome, were that everyone could indeed be a religious speaker, read the Bible, and have a personal relationship with God. In a sense, Jesus, Paul, and Luther had become the world's preeminent religious entrepreneurs, laying the foundation for broad innovation, creating numerous protestant creeds, and producing enormous swaths of individual religious freedoms.

The cultural superstructure was set. Individuals could set their own path to understanding God, a gigantic change of one's personal power over the Catholic autocratic tradition of sitting in church and having a priest tell you exactly what to think. The new religious marketplace produced three hundred years of warring factions, Protestants versus Catholic, when tens of thousands of people lost their lives because changes in kings and queens also led to changes of national faith and thus the deadly flushing out of those adhering to the *wrong* faith.

Imagine the accelerating freedoms of the Renaissance springing from the

Dark and Middle Ages when the church and king were the sole proprietors of ideas and power. Branches of government were forming, and the legislative and judicial branches were becoming more and more independent from the king. Laws existed, but not in the volume we see today. Commercial, contract and trade laws were lean. Western Civilization was finding very new legs. Trade produced wealth, not only for kings but an increasing large population of commoners as well. Capitalism was evolving from feudalism and mercantilism. Banks were forming. The first stock company was created, the Dutch East India Company. New wealth was not only invested in business ventures but also in art and science. Businesses flourished producing more employment and new streams of income for commoners. Culture and society evolved rapidly. Author Matt Ridley called the Renaissance a time when *ideas are having sex with ideas*. What an apt and lovely description of unrestrained and exponential idea creation.

The very basis for astronomical increases in idea generation resulted from an evolving understanding of property, of which ideas or intellectual property are a crucial component. Locke wrote about one's own body as the basis for individual property rights as well as the labor ensued from that body. Our mental labor, too, could be owned by a person as well as the capital that overlapped with new ideas.

Returning to the short definition from earlier in the book, *Capitalism is the intersection of ideas and capital.* When the sources of ideas can be from anyone and the sources of capital are broad—from one's personal savings account to a private investment firm—the proliferation of ideas, innovation and inventions are maximized. This describes the Renaissance. It also describes the cornucopia of innovations produced by America since its inception. In this century, though, the complexities and burdens issuing from our government and governments in the western world have hung a weight on idea creation. To return to the efficacy of the Renaissance, we need smarter, leaner, simpler, more entrepreneurial government that is a multiplier of ideas instead of the diminisher. New ideas solve problems; problems are not solved by old ideas repurposed by status quo government tacticians.

Beyond the economic benefit of Capitalism, our social and cultural lives are enriched by ideas. Going to a play, an art museum, joining a Rotary Club, or buying an iPhone is an opportunity to vote for or against a product, service, or solution. The great equalizer for Capitalism is not government nor the investor. The ultimate decider is the vote of consumers. We decide which automobiles are best, which religions, and which political candidates. The consumer has the ultimate power over how our economy, society, and culture work. In the twenty-first century, our vote is more important to businesses than ever. With tools for product feedback readily available to the browsing public, companies must compete with increasing diligence to acquire and retain our business. Think of your purchase of an iPhone over a Samsung, Chevy over Ford, or under Armour over Nike—consider how much time the consumer spends researching features and value for every purchase. Every decision is coupled to shopper ratings and competitive information. Every buying decision determines whether a product succeeds or fails and what companies remain in the competition and which are kicked to the curb. Capitalism is an economic, political, social, and cultural democracy of gigantic proportions in which your voting totals in the billions per day.

When investments increase, the number of entrepreneurs (i.e., new ideas) entering a marketplace or creating a new marketplace increases. The more entrepreneurial success a nation generates, the more wealth is created. Much of this wealth is invested in new ventures. The more income that is earned, the more jobs are created. The success of matching ideas and capital is directly proportional to economic freedom. Economic freedom is not only defined by your ability to vote for products; it is also defined by the freedom to conceive an idea, own it, and move it from conception to the marketplace with the leanest set of rules. When a nation allows an individual to own their intellectual property, a never-ending success cycle is initiated—idea, investment, industriousness, income and wealth; then more new ideas, innovation, and investment. The cycle can only be limited by government restrictions on our economic freedom. Restrictions occur every time a legislature writes new rules for economic transactions. When the rules plan for the competition, their results are vastly better than if they plan against competition.

Is America high on the global economic freedom list? It is, but, sadly, in this century it has fallen a few rungs down the ladder. Notably, China's position has improved, but it is still far behind America and the most western industrial nations. Conversely, because China's population is four times that of America, they need vastly less economic freedom to rise to first place. To counter China's giant population, incipient property rights and focus on Deng's path breakers, raising our economic freedom index should be an indispensable goal if America is to retain its leadership as the largest economy in the world. Raising our economic freedom index will also help ensure that America remains the most inviting economy for immigrant entrepreneurs to migrate to and start a business. America can only produce so many ideas because of the size of our population, and as there are eight billion potential idea generators around the world, adding idea generators via immigration should be a key goal for economic growth. Increasing economic freedom also ensures that America is a great setting for international private investment. Over the last decade, China's emerging economy has attracted far more investment than America. America needs to mitigate this liability to assure we are at parity with China for attracting private investment, noting that private investment and employment gains go hand in hand.

In a free market economy, competition assures that products and solutions constantly evolve, innovate, and improve as business competes for our consumption. Consumers vote to either sustain their existence or end it. Schumpeter proposed that some ideas are so new and disruptive that they replace aging ideas. Creative destruction, though frightening to many big business leaders, is crucial for optimized economic growth. American entrepreneurs destroyed old markets by creating new solutions: integrated circuits replaced vacuum tubes; cars replaced horse drawn carriages; light bulbs replaced candles . . . the list is grand and lengthy, and produced the greatest economy in the history of the world. In the twenty-first century, disruptive innovation is accelerating. The pace of innovation is five times faster this century than last. The Internet has opened a path for a vast swath of information technology, life science, and artificial intelligence entrepreneurs. Reiterating Easterly, lots of people creating lots of ideas, enhanced by broad economic and political freedoms, produce more and more private investment, which creates more ideas. Capitalism is an idea engine. Ideas are the fuel for economic growth.

The freer the society, the vaster the marketplace of ideas becomes, and not just business ideas. Most all our economic endeavors reveal a healthy, competitive marketplace. Science is a marketplace. Competing scientists race to be the first to validate a discovery. The competition is fierce. Art is a gigantic market. Religious markets struggle to compete for new parishioners. Capital is a market and an essential market at that. Immigration is a market with nations around the world competing for the best and brightest talent. Everything of value has a market, and every person in a free society is either adding ideas to the marketplace or voting on the solutions, or both. As we vote, ideas evolve and improve or stagnant and die.

Even politics is a quasi-market, albeit a closed duopoly, so new ideas do not readily flow into this marketplace; perhaps a bit of creative destruction or disruptive innovation would help!

Capitalism's Liabilities and Benefits

What are the liabilities of Capitalism? Economic growth ebbs and flows. Animal spirits have caused investors to create bubbles that burst and produce recessions and depressions. As the government has increased its regulatory powers over the last century with restrictive administrative regulations as well as economic throttles from the Federal Reserve, recessions, too, have been created by our government. The rich have gotten richer by their own conceits, but government has created as many problems as it has solved. Crony Capitalists add to the problem of government making the rich richer by planning against competition.

Has our government done a good job at the most important goal on its Capitalist responsibility list: Containing greed? Since large corporations spent over $3 billion dollars to get Congress to pass laws that protect their businesses or minimize competition and taxation, *maybe not*. On the other hand, Americans should be thanked. Greedy Capitalists tend not to provide the best products, so we tend not to vote for those companies and their products. We show them the economic exit. Considering the number of votes we cast each day for products, the number of bad purchases is extremely low, and the chances of running into a bad player in the course of our daily consumption is even lower because the number of good choices we make is quite large. In one way, Capitalism matured with the inclusion of the Internet in our everyday lives, as the amount of research on products, including customer feedback, has improved our buying investments. Though the Internet has vastly increased our productivity, it too has liabilities that challenge us, but as the market evolves, and we evolve, the blemishes will ultimately decline.

Capitalism's key benefit is, then—it is a maximizer of ideas, limited only when government executes law and regulation in ways that diminish economic freedom, reduce competition, or create compliance costs that are out of proportion to their benefit. In some cases, these restrictions are caused by needless complexity. More often the objective is the desire for political power. For the Left, the restrictions are deliberate and burdensome because of a lack of trust in both themselves and the people they lead. For Capitalists in business and politics, assuring the status quo and protecting commercial treasures hurt America's ability to innovate and grow.

Conclusions

More Schumpeter: *"Can capitalism survive? No. I do not think it can."* Given the spectacular results of Capitalism and of entrepreneurial creative destruction, of new markets for cars, planes, electricity and other products that created vast increases in productivity, one wonders if what Schumpeter really meant was *Can capitalism survive in its current state?* His *No* has been proved wrong by the Chinese and every nation on earth that has sought to improve its economic freedom through improving property rights, encouraging well-regulated banking, and integrating free trade among many variables for economic freedom. This is reminiscent of a quote from Monty Python's *In Search of the Holy Grail* when a character being carried off to the cemetery is asked if he is dead, and responds, "I'm not dead, yet." It's hard to kill any idea, good or bad, as evolution erases old scars, but Capitalism continues to live and evolve.

Socialist economies, like Red China or the USSR, suffered from two massive problems: lack of new ideas handicapped by lack of property rights which translated to the inability to create new ideas, and the failure to derive wealth from those ideas that could be reinvested in the economy. The innovation engine was stunted from a person's ability to own their own labor and ideas. No fuel for the engine.

The Socialist approach exploited by many western nations has the same problem in smaller portions. As the government takes over the means of production via social monopolies or private enterprise, the evolution of ideas for those monopolies is severely minimized capturing institutions and programs in the status quo. As the Socialist approach requires no financial reports of what success is, the success or failure of social outcomes are not measured but simply ignored in favor of public greed (bigger budgets). Government becomes an ever-increasing tax on our nation's overall productivity; devolving the idea engine devolves.

Are social monopolies needed from time to time, despite these challenges? Certainly, especially to ensure those in most need have some safety net. More on how this can be accomplished will be discussed later in this book in, *"What's the Plan?"*

Whereas Socialism is a diminisher of ideas, Capitalism is an idea and innovation engine, and not just for commercial markets but for any market: culture, social, arts, economics, and sciences. Capital in Capitalism is also because it is a market, and like all markets it continues to evolve and improve with time albeit with an occasional mole that needs to be excised. Socialism and the Socialist approach get stuck in their ideological concrete and their stagnating, unchanging government monopolies.

A Note on Innovation and Legislative Restraint

Great care is required to write law. Whether the Socialist's approach or the Capitalist's, our government's legislative processes and generation of law are complex and confusing and most legislators do not have a chance to read the laws they pass, much less understand the contents or implications of their endeavors. Even sausage-making looks cleaner and smarter. There appears to be no restraint regarding complexity and no priority for simplicity in legislation or regulation. During this century, the appeal of complexity has intensified.

The more laws politicians write, the fewer the rights we enjoy. Consider speed limits. The first limits for autos arrived in 1901 in Connecticut: twelve mph in the city, fifteen mph outside the city. Prior to 1901, an auto could travel freely at any speed. Was a law really needed? It was needed if you wanted to make sure autos didn't spook the horses on the streets. On the legislative upside, signed speed limits are the epitome of simplicity. It's not that rules and regulations are not required. It's how the rules are written that either are simple to understand and obey, and—for business—whether rules encourage the creation of ideas or cripple them. If voters had the time to read our Federal Registry of laws to find legislation that promoted idea creation, examples would be slim to none. Finding laws or regs that are easy to understand are also AWOL.

The best example of simplicity and restraint is found in the Bill of Rights. The first amendment begins with five words that should be guidance of our legislators: "Congress shall make no law." Most laws are lists of items of what Americans can or cannot do. Lists can be exceedingly long and exceedingly complex. Most recently both Obamacare and Dodd–Frank Wall Street Reform and Consumer Protection Act exceeded 20,000 pages. These laws and the tens of thousands of pages of federal laws and regulations already in the Federal Register have pushed compliance costs to nearly 10 percent of our GDP, an extraordinary cost. Making no law translates into no restraints of our freedom. But no law is anarchy. Law is required. It must be simple, however. Consider that the first amendment contains only forty-five words, but it shows economy of words with extraordinary power for citizens.

That some rules are needed, the challenge for creating effective rules is two-fold. First, Socialist problem-solving produces big federal monopolies whose operational instructions need to be written down so federal employees can execute the desire of Congress—no easy task. Second, the legal profession is a purveyor, by its very nature, of complexity. Because a majority of our federal representatives are lawyers, restraint for these complexity-minded professionals is no easy task. Rules should be explicit enough to keep everyone inside the lines—but simple enough for the typical person (especially entrepreneurs) to understand without needing a lawyer. In both cases, Socialist or legalistic, rules are written to be restrictive, legally confusing, and inflexible. This approach is at odds with government that needs to be evolutionary, innovative, and, on occasion, creatively destructive.

Was this complex approach always inherent in our government? Not really. In fact, our government was expressly constructed with limited responsibilities, a limited federal government. At the beginning of the twentieth century, only a few dozen federal laws filled the Federal Register. Now there are thousands. Until the 1936 Supreme Court's Helverling v Davis decision—allowing a new tax to collect revenues for social security, spending that was outside constitutional authority government's tentacles were limited by the constitution's general welfare clause and the specific tasks it assigned to the legislature. Justice Benjamin CardozoCardozo, writing for the Court's majority, changed the breadth of our limited federal government to a strong central government. He wrote: *"Congress may spend money in aid of the "general welfare." There have been great statesmen in our history who have stood for other views. We will not resurrect the contest. It is now settled by decision. The conception of the spending power advocated by Hamilton and strongly reinforced by Story has prevailed over that of Madison which has not been lacking in adherents."*

In short, he abandoned our constitution's original spending limits and allowed Congress to spend money on anything for any reason, without limit. Whether Cardozo's intent was to allow a Socialist bent to our government, the court's decision provided the superstructure for Socialists to erect social monopolies. This new freedom for the government may have sounded good to many on the Left at the time. Time, however, has produced a heavy avalanche of newly acquired government powers and restrictions for its citizens in the name of good intentions. Could these new social monopolies have been written in a way that encouraged new ideas and allowed for an evolution of the operation of these programs to assure they met social goals and financial sustainability? Absolutely. Is there a path where programs might suffer creative destruction with the erection of transformative new solutions? There is. Government, however, is set up like old industrialists who loved their powerful corporations and would do anything to stamp out competition from new entrepreneurs with new solutions that might replace their industry. The translation? There is little desire for restraint among our leaders. They love the power that law, money and the status quo provide them.

Given the approach to big, complex social programs and an administrative state that our leaders have continued to expand in complexity, in cost, and in populations served, the restraint—that should be a component for leadership of any organization, but especially for government—has been lost. Instead of finding solutions that minimized cost and maximized results, government provided minimal results for maximum costs; then, when financial challenges arrived, politicians requested more money, more taxes, and more expansive reach of programs. Instead of applying critical thinking, this is government by goofy, or Goofy. The gravity of power is the great diminisher of wisdom.

Our retirement system is a great example. When Social Security and Medicare were launched in 1936 and 1967 respectively, both programs targeted the poor. This system worked well to help the poor without busting the bank. Today, every citizen is enrolled. Instead of the original rate of retirement taxes of about 2 percent, today they are 15.3 percent, and the system is unfunded to the tune of $100 trillion. No restraint. When solutions, like our retirement systems, trend badly, instead of fixing the system, our leaders expand it and increase taxes.

This strategy not only lacks restraint; it erases common sense and obliterates critical thinking. Transformations that could fix our national social framework are routinely dispatched by angry partisanship and anti-intellectual (but remarkably effective) political advertising.

Voter beware. Expanding the status quo this century will be an extremely dangerous game for our children's livelihoods and will give the reins of power to China.

MARKETS VERSUS MONOPOLIES

"Markets change, tastes change, so the companies and the individuals who choose to compete in those markets must change."
An Wang, Founder of Wang Computers

"Government is the ultimate monopoly. And monopolies, as any economist will tell you, often breed complacency and a lack of innovation."
Gavin Newsom, Governor of California

MOST OF US HAVE AN appreciation for markets as something not unlike the market where we get groceries. Consumers want loads of products, numerous choices, and a variety of vendors competing for our business. Our supermarkets are one of many markets across a vast menu of industries: auto, truck, food, clothes, computers, Internet, media, news, banking, capital, communications—even our labor and ideas exist in a marketplace. Each industry has multiple vendors; each vendor has more than a few products. Broader marketplaces are local, regional and international.

Investopedia defines a market economy as, "an economic system in which economic decisions and the pricing of goods and services are guided by the interactions of a country's individual citizens and businesses." The market in a market economy traces back to the first economic transaction, before money existed to value transactions. Bartering a goat for corn, or tin for leather established pricing on a transaction-by-transaction basis. Price discovery was no easy task and it changed with every transaction. With the advent of farming, animal husbandry and coinage, small cities formed and bazaars in the middle east arrived where excess production of anything was for sale. Negotiations for price were still transactional but coinage helped. These early instances of markets were the beginnings of a long evolution to Capitalism and free enterprise as well as for Socialist and government-driven, but less open markets.

Today's markets are not unlike historical, middle eastern bazaars. The modern versions are swap meets and yard sales which survive in every city and most neighborhoods. Electronically, eBay is a web swap meet that extends from local, to national, to international arenas. Amazon is the most all-encompassing marketplace in history. Pricing, even for Amazon, is still based on individual transactions, but transactions that occur in the thousands or millions. The same transactional pricing occurs in business markets where transactions are aggregated by enterprises to understand when prices need to be reduced, to turn inventory, or increased because there is too little supply for market demands. Every transaction is a vote for or against a product, for or against the current price, or, on occasion, as conspicuous consumption exists, regardless of price.

Markets are evolutionary because they are competitive. For every idea generated and launched as a business, new ideas follow from competitors with improved pricing and features. Leaders in competing businesses work diligently to reduce costs of production as well as focus to improve products with features customers seek. For every market, a creative destructor eventually unveils an innovative solution that craters old market players, the new market absorbing the clientele of the old market. For instance, computers largely replaced typewriters.

Markets are fluid and evolutionary. When capital is available, markets proliferate ideas. As capital is also a market and seeker of new ideas, the two rely on one another for future economic success. The more open and free the marketplace of ideas and capital markets, the more ideas reach the consumer, and the more likely it is that products will improve in quality, feature, and price.

Markets are the ultimate idea funnel. A flood of ideas arrive at the top of the funnel, and only the best come out the narrow end. As ideas are the currency of economic success and markets are the deployer of new ideas, both are essential to a well-run, growing economy.

Like markets, monopolies have ancient beginnings. Kings, queens, dictators, and religious leaders owned almost everything. They had an ultimate monopoly on power, gold, ideas, and land, which was for millennia nearly everything.

A litany of economic papers has been published stating that monopolies, both government and commercial, are not necessarily harmful, nor do they produce unfair pricing because of their dominance in the market they rule. Against this setting, competing research focusing on commercial entities paints a different story painting the pricing advantage of monopolies as problematic. The problems of monopolies or near monopolies, though, reach further than pricing. Public monopolies reduce innovation as they create high barriers to market entries or alternatives, obviating competition and killing new ideas.

Near monopolies like Microsoft, Facebook, and Google provide services that are affordable and well used by the vast majority of consumers. On the other hand, their political clout is a constant thorn in Washington's side and their leaders have been dragged in front of Congressional committees to answer questions about content bias and misuse of economic power. Political power overshadows the pricing gentility of these organizations though they do not quite reach the status of monopoly.

The economic history of America contains only a few commercial monopolies. America's economic runup in the late 1800s produced several corporate titans that spurred the passage of the Sherman Anti-trust laws in 1890, which ultimately dismantled Standard Oil and American Tobacco in the early 1900s. In the twentieth century, a private/public monopoly crossbreed, AT&T, a government built and highly regulated utility that was also traded on the DOW Industrials, was dismantled in the 1980s. Might big tech follow the fate of AT&T and Standard Oil. It is possible. And what about monopolies erected by the government for schools, health care, and retirement. These appear to be immune to anti-trust laws and to exist under the legal monopoly erected by government itself!

Commercial businesses that gain exceptionally large market share can produce solutions at a lower cost than competition, mostly because of scale and efficiencies that may be hard for smaller competitors to duplicate. Government's job is to assure that competitive and/or disruptive entrees into the marketplace do not meet anti-competitive barriers generated by big economic players and their lobbyists, creating monopoly-like conditions that establish regulatory barriers to entry that stifle competition.

Though monopolies in the commercial markets should always be concerning, the bigger economic challenge is government monopolies, especially at the federal level. The effectiveness of government social monopolies has diminished over time and costs have outpaced value and results. Could the government break up these monopolies? The government can do what it pleases, but the political will does not exist as vast pools of political power depend on their permanence. A sage aphorism about government programs is that once invented, they are immortal. Ronald Reagan said, "No government ever voluntarily reduces itself in size. Government programs, once launched, never disappear. Actually, a government bureau is the nearest thing to eternal life we'll ever see on this earth!" Evolution of new ideas for poorly performing public monopolies is unlikely short of a total financial catastrophe, and even then, change is unlikely.

As Governor Newsom stated above, government, by definition, is a monopoly. The FBI must be the enforcer of federal laws and owns this marketplace of federal law enforcement. The treasury must be *the* single provider of our currency. The same is true for the military, the judiciary, and the short list of other constitutional responsibilities. The limits that the founding fathers placed on the government's responsibilities were very much about assuring that the government would not become too powerful and usurp our individual rights. The line between the federal government's responsibilities and the power of the states is also well defined.

The responsibilities of each branch are finely delineated in the Constitution and the Bill of Rights. The Tenth Amendment tacks on a poignant exclamation mark: "*The powers not delegated to the United States by the Constitution, nor prohibited by it to the States, are reserved to the States respectively, or to the people.*" The consequences of these limits, which have been horribly abused by Congress and presidents over the last ten decades, should be heeded as each new government monopoly to dispense services limits our choices and diminishes our productivity. Most economists note that government is a tax on our productivity. The bigger the government, the larger the hit to productivity. Regardless of the government getting outside the lines of its constitutional responsibilities, its institutions are government monopolies, and this structure is essential. Government inspired social monopolies, however, present a problem, as they are dispensing products and services and seldom provide positive social or financial returns.

Because the government owns the means of production for social monopolies, it also owns and creates the legal strictures for the operation of monopolies. Because government owns both the means of production and legislative responsibility, the Socialist approach is highly autocratic, not unlike the prerogatives of kings and popes. Imagine if Google owned both the market for Search and Ads but also wrote the federal laws governing these services. This is precisely what government does. Government's dual prerogatives ensures there is no separation of authority between production and legislation, so political processes become protective of the monopolies' long-term existence—at all costs. To further protect these monopolies, monied interests—whether unions, business, or special interests—lobby to guarantee continued existence of these monopolies even when the results are poor. Political power trumps common sense. Social monopolies exist in the shadows and are a terribly abused conflict of interest whose inadequate results fall heavily on the poor.

Like monopolies, government program accountability for pricing and value is not a concern as it would be for competitors in a marketplace. When prices and costs are out of kilter, Congress asks for more money. The value between price and quality is replaced by political will and the propensity to acquire votes, a political decision versus a decision based on merit.

Conversely, tech giants, like Google, spend heavily on lobbying, but they do not own the right to create the laws they may desire. They influence the legislature but do not own the process. Sadly, big money does heavily influence the legislative processes. Crony Capitalism for both the Capitalist Google and the Socialist approach to public education are both flavors of Socialism. Regardless of Google's lobbying, however, there is separation of authority and delegation of duty for business execution and legislative responsibility.

Though the line between private business execution becomes hazy with huge political donations and large investments in lobbying, a clear line identifies separates business responsibilities and those that belong to government. This is not the case with government's social monopolies.

Public education provides a great example. Legislative responsibilities as well as the execution of education services are functions of government, without separation of duties or delegation of authority to parents. Legal barriers are instituted to protect the monopoly. With the assistance of unions, whose existence fully relies on continued government ownership, and which uses dues from employees who have the same vested interest in continued government ownership, competition is stifled. Though private, religious, and charter options exist, their market share is minimized by rules that mitigate broader expansion, especially for charters.

The education monopoly is a double anti-competitive whammy as monopoly pricing is on a constant rise and quality has decreased over the last six decades.

A third barrier to education success is the Socialist top-down habit of stifling innovation. For example, after fifty years of central planning efforts to increase the quality in public schools, the top-down has not one win. Failures include busing, equalization of per-pupil spending, Title IX regulations, No Child Left Behind, Common Core, and others. After sixty years of the one-size-fits-all approach, the cost of education per pupil in real dollars has doubled, and yet the proficiency of students according to the National Assessment Educational Progress is flat to slightly down during the same period. Why? No competition. No new ideas. Our educational system is stuck in the 1930s and it is 2020.

Commercial and government monopolies alike wrap themselves in their original blanket of success and then protect that paradigm at all costs. This approach had only some efficacy when the pace of change was measured by the century or scores of years. When the pace of change is every few years, and accelerating, social monopolies have become a giant anchor on our personal, corporate, government, and overall national success.

Could the expansion of public and private markets for education improve education? It should at least be tested. Could our retirement system fix its $100 trillion underfunding by taking advantage of personal savings and investment and by retargeting retirement to focus on those who are poor and in greatest need of assistance? Could we transform the War on Poverty to a set of solutions that focus on human capital investment instead of transferring payments to individuals, reducing poverty? Sure. The how-to is the challenge, but more on this later.

There should be no doubt in the reader's mind that the government occasionally needs to intrude to fix a problem with a Socialist/monopolistic approach. What is missing is a planned exit strategy to move to a market solution or a better designed monopoly, if and/or when the results are not satisfactory.

Objectives should be set as to what results are great or good versus poor or adequate; then when goals are missing, change is mandated.

Conclusion

Markets have three grand advantages over monopolies. First, they are vastly more efficient because competition mandates efficiency to gain success with consumers. Second, markets are more effective, producing better results as successful companies listen to customer feedback to improve products. Third, markets are an idea engine when sound capital markets exist and property rights are well protected. When the marketplace of ideas is open to all, and capital is available, products and markets continually expand and evolve. Whereas monopolies are one size, and all solutions are built on a seldom changing foundation, markets are based on millions or billions of inputs from consumers and inventors, where vast swaths of transactions inform the market each day, and each day the market evolves to a new set of ideas that aim at constant improvement.

Private or public monopolies are idea killers as competition is stifled and ideas are diminished. The Socialist approach to governance is sometimes necessary but should always be used with caution as social monopolies should never be forever.

TO PROFIT OR NOT TO PROFIT

"To profit without risk, experience without
danger, and reward without work, is as impossible
as it is to live without being born."
A. P. Gouthev

OVER THE LAST FEW DECADES, the notion of profits has fared poorly with social justice warriors around the world. For the great unwashed masses who
may be unfamiliar with social justice, or what it means, the *social* in social
justice is a derivative of Socialist philosophy, not being social on the Internet.
Social justice warriors dislike profits which are a byproduct of their dislike of
Capitalism, the lineage of which derives directly from Marx.

> This boundless greed after riches, this passionate chase after exchange-
> value, is common to the capitalist and the miser; but while the miser
> is merely a capitalist gone mad, the capitalist is a rational miser. The
> never-ending augmentation of exchange-value, which the miser strives
> after, by seeking to save his money from circulation, is attained by the
> more acute capitalist, by constantly throwing it afresh into circulation.
> Marx, Karl. Das Kapital - Capital: Best Online Edition (Kindle Location
> 2953). Kindle Edition.

The quote beckons the distasteful flavor left on our economic psyche by
the miserly Scrooge in Charles Dickens's *A Christmas Carol*, published twenty years before Marx's Communist digest. Scrooge is certainly a person we
all love to dislike, as well as, after his redemption, a person we tend to appreciate. The untold Scrooge story, however, is that all the money he saved, with
little spent on himself or his employees, was housed in a bank that likely did
use that capital for other local ventures producing jobs and income and maybe
a bit of wealth for those concerned on both ends of the investment. There are
scrooges in modern Capitalism, but most do one thing well that government
cannot; they invest in the economy to encourage new ideas which create new
jobs, income, and more wealth—by risking their *own* dollars. Because they

have skin in the game, they invest with wisdom the politician cannot match, as the money the politician spends is more of an expenditure of 'other people's money' rather than a personal investment. Good intentions may exist but are generally less important than political will or power. Worse, dollars spent are not the legislators, but yours; any risk in spending is on our shoulders, not the politicians. No matter how much is spent, there is no risk to the political spender. Big spending is well protected by big campaign contributors, and it is an incentive to acquire votes.

For Marx, profits were unpaid wages to the worker. The existence of profits means the worker was not paid the value he put into the product from his labor. From the Left's perspective, businesses that produce profit are bad because they steal from the worker. Their conclusion: Because government has no profits, it must be good. The presumption is that profits corrupt business, but even bigger money (tax revenues and government spending) does not corrupt politics. That the typical Fortune 500 company averages about $20 billion in revenues and our federal government's spending total $4.8 trillion in 2020, and, if power is money, and money corrupts, then the problem with government corruption is worse by nearly 250 times.

Most of us understand the potential for corruption in businesses and government, and the greed of players in both enterprises. Though there may be disdain for profits, few consumers seek products and services from companies that are unprofitable or that have fallen from our favor with bad business practices. The voter also tacitly understands the corruption of our politicians and bureaucrats, as 80 percent of us distrust government.

From *Oxford Dictionary,* Profit: a financial gain, especially the difference between the amount earned and the amount spent in buying, operating, or producing something.

Though one's home budget is not a business budget, personal budgets are an analog to business income and expense statements and help define why profits matter.

A worker's labor has value that is transmitted via a paycheck. Depending on the type of skills a job requires and the willingness of the worker to work, one's labor determines the size of the check. If the worker is married, the spouse's labor adds to the monthly revenue. One's bills are like the expenses of a business. When family expenses are subtracted, rent/mortgage, electricity, water, food, clothes, and taxes are deducted from income, disposable income results. For many of us, there is little or no disposable income at the end of the month. When there is a bit left over, these dollars are discretionary spending, or, if not spent, they are saved. These could as easily be named *your personal profit*. The worker owns this profit, not the government. When we have extra dollars, it is a good thing, an incredibly good thing! Ditto for business.

Schumpeter and the Entrepreneur

Entrepreneurs are the exemplars of how even the simplest idea, from the simplest person, finds a market that produces income and perhaps a bit of wealth. Schumpeter states:

> I will not stay to stress, though I must mention, that even the classical theory is not as wrong as Marx pretended it was. "Saving up" in the most literal sense has been, especially in earlier stages of Capitalism, a not unimportant method of "original accumulation." Moreover, there was another method that was akin to it though not identical with Many a factory in the seventeenth and eighteenth centuries was just a shed that a man was able to put up by the work of his hands and required only the simplest equipment to work it. In such cases the manual work of the prospective capitalist plus a quite small fund of savings was all that was needed—and brains, of course.] Schumpeter, Joseph. Capitalism, Socialism, and Democracy (Kindle Locations 387-392). Start Publishing LLC. Kindle Edition.

Like the home budget and its hope for a little discretionary spending, a new small business is generally formed by a couple of lonely guys in the garage like Steve Jobs and Steve Wozniak who hope to make enough money to sell their product and have some dollars left over to eat and live. Apple's initial capital came from factoring an order placed by an electronics store that wanted to buy the first fifty Apple computers. What followed from these fifty computers, was a successful business startup, going to a nearly-out-of-money corporation in the early part of this century, and going on to a trillion-dollar corporate valuation today. Every big company started as a small enterprise that possessed a great idea that intersected with capital. Once that idea is placed in motion, consumers start voting with their pocketbooks.

Apple's scorecard: from two employees to 147,000. Average employee pay is over $125,000. When Apple went public, forty of its employees became overnight millionaires, and vastly more since. A $1,000 investment in the IPO is now worth $430,000. Millions of citizens own a piece of Apple. Regarding profits, according to the website Statistica, "Apple reported net income of 57.41 billion U.S. dollars in its 2020 fiscal year, the second highest net income to date. Apple's global revenue rose to 274.52 billion U.S. dollars in that same year." Apple banked nearly $200 billion in cash reserves which it reinvests in its business, other businesses and even in U.S. government bonds. As a percentage, their profits were about 21 percent of revenue. These numbers are not just good; they are great, and Apple has achieved this success year after year for at least a decade. With profits like these, do consumers think they are greedy? It appears not.

The tech sector over the last many decades has story after story about one or a couple of guys/gals with ideas who start a business and rise to the pinnacle of financial success and great profitability. And they all reinvested the corporate profits to scale their businesses and improve their products so consumers would continue to invest precious dollars in their products. Did a few CEOs buy yachts, houses in the south of France, and a Maserati? Yep, and good for them. On the flip side, they invested billions in new ventures and billions more on charitable ventures. Good for us. Without profits not only do their investments in business and charity vanish, so too do their companies. Without quality profits, Apple would still be working out of a garage in California.

Schumpeter's belief in the importance of entrepreneurs is sometimes lost in the haze of political wonks and financial media's heavy focus on the demand side of the economy and large Fortune 1000 businesses. Throughout history, a cornucopia of entrepreneurs created ideas that improved or created markets, starting with fire, the wheel and agriculture, to the steam engine and cotton gin, to electricity, cars, and airplanes, to today's the iPhone, Google search, and Microsoft Office. Had none of these innovations attracted capital produced from other people's profits, we would all be living in a tent and scarfing nuts from trees. Profits, personal or otherwise, drive innovation and jobs. For hundreds of thousands of entrepreneurs, personal savings funded their new businesses. Though there may be a few miserly Scrooges hording their money for their own benefit, their cohort is tiny.

Soldiers coming home from World War II offer a great example of how savings drive job creation. When World War II ended, most every economist believed that ten million servicemen coming home from the war would create a recession that might create another depression. Few considered that most servicemen were saving their paychecks. There were not many venues to spend money at the war front. According to *US Veterans Magazine,* fifty percent of those exiting the military started businesses with their savings. People that had been through the worst possible times, the greatest hardships imaginable, stepped happily into the freest nation in the world and did what most people would not do, ever! They took a dive into business and controlled their own destiny. If the Germans could not kill them, then anything was possible. These brave warriors created a gigantic economic wave.

For Schumpeter and most liberal economists, profits result from financial risk taken when using capital to invest in a new venture or to reinvest in current business. For a well-run business, investments create growth, jobs, and more profit that can be reinvested.

Not all profits when reinvested create a positive return on investment. Some companies use their capital poorly or miss innovation opportunities that their competition launches and wind up losing their business. Companies come and go depending on their ability to invest in ways that delight their customers sufficiently to purchase their products again and again. That's the risk one takes with investments, whether using one's own money or money from other private sources. Risk is a key variable in the value of the investment. When there is no risk, like a savings account, the consumer gets a 1 percent return. As risk increases, the potential for greater return increases. The possibility for failure also rises.

Some profits are labeled obscene while others seem to pass some unwritten seal of approval. For instance, Apple is one of the most profitable companies in the world. As noted above, Apple reported net income of $57.41 billion in 2020 on revenues of $274.52 billion, or 21 percent of revenue. Exxon, however, is reviled by the Left because their product produces carbon dioxide emissions. Exxon's profits were $14.3 billion on $243 billion in revenues or

5.8 percent of revenue. Yet Exxon profits are reviled, while Apple's are loved? The politics behind carbon dioxide color the disfavor offered Exxon by the Left. Is it fair? Of course, it is. It's politics. Everything is fair game. But is it reasonable, regarding the value of profits? Probably not. There is no replacement energy (yet) for oil and when some entrepreneurial scientist discovers a new fuel source that will electrify cars inexpensively, oil will become a thing of the past. Until then, should one consider Apple's 21 percent or Exxon's 5.8 percent profitability obscene. To that, the answer is, "No" as long as people will pay a premium price for Apple's products or a commodity price for filling your car's tank; hundreds of millions of consumers do both happily.

The Socialist approach to profits fails because investments by government carry no risk for the leaders recommending the investment. Whether the investment is in Solyndra, or Tesla tax-credits for wealthy buyers, or our investment in an ineffective education system, there is no blow back to the persons (our leaders) making decisions about the investment even if that investment does not work over decades. Few if any political entrepreneurs are recommending transformational changes that involve Schumpeter's creative destruction. There are only continual requests for more money despite poor results. Worse, as a nonprofit, the government's income statement should show that tax revenues equal government spending, but the government borrowing is growing into the trillions a year—to pay for investments that have a negative return on investment. How well our pols invest is vastly more important than how much one spends, especially if the spending does not have a positive effect. The blowback for poor investing is obviated in that there is no government dashboard reporting government investment successes or failures. There is no single source of the truth because information is dark.

With information starvation, not only can government not create a profit, which is reasonable for a nonprofit organization, but politicians seem not to care a whit whether it produces a positive result for the dollars the voter provides in taxes. Spending decisions are political, not financial. Results are reported partisan-spun, not based on social results. Schools that educate everyone to proficiency would have grand social and financial payback, but only 1/3 of students obtain a quality education. The War on Poverty would have huge financial implications for this century if *The War* reduced poverty. Our retirement system could produce trillions in individual savings and invest-ments, but it remains a tax-based system that will continue to be underfunded up to $100 trillion through the rest of the century. Even nonprofits, like gov-ernment, need to produce value, and like businesses where profits are a mea-sure of success, the government needs to measure the *value* of spending—not *how much* was spent.

Measure of Success

Profits are a measure of value to the consumer. Marx marveled at Capitalism's ability to create *"more massive and more colossal productive forces than have all preceding generations together . . ."* This occurred be-cause the individual freedom to own ideas and for those ideas to produce more than a dollar of value for each dollar invested, produced a profit. Marx similarly worried about the amazing efficiency of Capitalists. The constant focus on reducing costs and on improving process, both of which increased profits, also improved price and quality. He feared Capitalism's focus on ef-ficiency would also reduce the pay of workers to zero, a not unreasonable consideration for the time. Another economist who shared the same concern, Alfred Marshall, took to the streets of London to find evidence of whether the devolution of labor value was indeed decreasing. The following is from Sylvia Nasar's excellent history of economics, the *Grand Pursuit*.

> *He did not doubt that the chief cause of poverty was low wages, but what caused wages to be low. ... He cited as evident the fact that, con-trary to Marx's claim that competition would cause wages of skilled and unskilled workers to converge near subsistence level, skilled workers were earning 'two, three, four times' as much as unskilled laborers. The fact that employers were willing to pay more for specialized training for skill implied that wages depended on workers' contribution to current output. Or, put another way, that the demand for labor, not only the sup-ply, helped to determine pay. ... As technology, education, and improve-ments in organization increased productivity over time, the income of the working classes would rise in tandem.*

Nasar provides more of Marshall's insight on wages from his *Lectures to Women:*

> *There are I believe in the world few things with greater capability of poetry in it that the multiplication table…If you can get mental and moral capital to grow at some rate per annum there is no limit to advance that may be made; if you can give it the vital force which will make the multiplication table applicable to it, it becomes a little seed that will grow up to a tree of boundless size. (IBID)*

Low income, then and now, is not because of low wages; low wages result from lack of human capital. When human capital increases with education and, for Marshall, in on-the-job experience, wages rise, and this is precisely why England had the highest wages in Europe at the time.

Finally, profits are the essential measure of the sustainability of a business, both in Capitalist and Socialist terms. Every successful product produces benefit for the purchaser, or it ceases to exist. The more benefit, the better. Consumers, not government, determine the value of the benefit by determining the price of the product and the value to the owner. Do consumers pay a premium for an iPhone. Yes, they do, and few, if any, complain as the benefits are enormous. The same is true of the cars we buy, clothes, food, everything, even gasoline. Even software! Microsoft CEO Satya Nadella framed what the responsibilities of his business were with respect to social justice.

During an interview at the Economic Policy Research Summit:

> Jeff Raikes asked, "Let's talk a little bit more about equity. Before the pandemic, the world was facing big challenges: climate change, structural racism, economic insecurity, wealth inequality and more. What is the responsibility of the corporations, particularly the underlying connection to racial justice in the U.S. and elsewhere?"

> Nadella: "the social purpose of a company is to find profitable solutions to the challenges of people and planet… Driving broad economic growth is perhaps the biggest thing that a company can do in order to have the pie distributed evenly, the pie should first grow."

The software corporation for which I worked had much the same view of our mission—to make every business in the world run better. This is the uniform focus of almost every technology company, providing innovation that reduces the costs of doing business by helping employees do their jobs more efficiently and with better insight. And not just the technology industry. The farmer, the industrialist, the auto maker, the playwright, the candlestick maker and Smith's butcher. Justice, both individual, corporate and social, is a derivative of our collective desire to improve our lives with our skills and capabilities and ideas.

Conclusions

Profits are a measure of the personal, social and corporate value and success. Profits are not in themselves, good or bad. However, profits that are ill gotten must be, and generally are, excised from the system. Can profits be excessive? Probably not, if only because this means that consumers are willing to pay an excessive price for the product like the iPhone. Excessive pricing, though, is not sustainable. If price and value are out of sync, businesses fail.

Regarding nonprofits, especially our government, our biggest challenge is that Americans are paying an excessive price for government because spending is executed via partisan political decisions, not by discovery of positive financial and social solutions. Businesses and their profits are evidence based, not unlike how scientists prove theories. Partisan politics is not about the data, nor the evidence, or good results. It's about power, pure and simple. Congresses and presidents could take a lesson from the chief financial officers about successful investment of every dollar spent and the continuous effort to report on those investments.

FREEDOM VERSUS EQUALITY

*"Rightful liberty is unobstructed action according to our
will within limits drawn around us by the equal rights
of others. I do not add 'within the limits of the law'
because law is often but the tyrant's will, and always
so when it violates the rights of the individual."*
Thomas Jefferson

*"Freedom is the catalyst of greatness
in all human endeavors."*
Tom Lewellen

FAMED ECONOMIST AND NOBEL LAUREATE Martin Friedman captured the tension between these pivotal words that shape American Democracy and liberal economics (capitalism):

"A society that puts equality before freedom will get neither. A society that puts freedom before equality will get a high degree of both."

How our political leaders treat this tension defines the very underpinnings of each political party's approach to governance. As Democrats have aligned with egalitarianism (i.e. the Socialist approach), Republicans have focused on individual liberty, the Capitalist approach, though each party sometimes loses focus.

The Declaration of Independence gives light to equality and the basis or our democratic values.

*We hold these truths to be self-evident, that all men are created equal,
that they are endowed by their Creator with certain unalienable Rights,
that among these are Life, Liberty and the pursuit of Happiness.--That
to secure these rights, Governments are instituted among Men, deriving
their just powers from the consent of the governed . . .*

The key word in the phrase is 'created.' We are equal before the law, but our life, liberty and pursuit of happiness is a journey of our own making. Jefferson lamented that governments by their very nature grew more and more powerful and more and more complex with time. It's what governments do, and for that matter, what every organization does. Bigger is not always better and governments, because they are a tax on our production, should take care to minimize their girth while maximizing their effectiveness. On every occasion when legislators write law, our freedoms diminish, and government grows stronger. When government absorbs our responsibilities, our freedoms are reduced. When the government owns the means of production, the Socialist approach, our freedoms shrink.

The mission of the Socialist approach is to legislate our rights and to mandate legal enforcement. This approach when confined to criminal law and constitution law works wells. Catching and jailing a criminal requires laws that are very specific, so criminals do not drop through the cracks. We would all hope to be treated equally in a criminal trial with laws being applied uniformly to all. When equality is applied to products and services are delivered by government, when more and more products and services are delivered by government, our freedoms are hemmed in, and our choices are limited to one choice and the vast complexity of rules for the monopoly. This egalitarian approach is the western approach to Socialism where freedoms or rights are legislated by government and *owned by government*. The right to an education for our children is owned by the government. We have no freedom of choice. The right to a retirement check and retirement health care are owned and limited by the government. The way we finance our private health care via our employers is highly regulated by government to the point there is only a single insurance option: an HMO/PPO, the most expensive option to insure health care. Because of the high expense, the right to buy insurance is severely limited by government.

Friedman's quote goes to point. The more government attempts to equalize social or economic outcomes, the more government socializes outcomes (now called *equity*), the more our freedom is reduced and as costs increase, quality and value decrease.

Freedom is the catalyst to greatness. The freer we are, the more likely our potential for success will be realized. Freedom is not always easy. Freedom is sometimes a messy process, but freedom that increases our choices produces incredibly good outcomes. When allowed to vote politically, economically, socially and culturally, our freedom produces amazing results.

Only the wisest of leaders will understand how to legislate without diminishing our freedoms. A leader should be a multiplier of our individual freedoms, not a diminisher. Those who preach equality in situations outside our legal rights are purveyors of unfreedom.

The freer our speech, the better our understanding of the world around us, and the more expansive the marketplace of ideas expands, regardless of the marketplace—political, economic, social and cultural, the better our paths for greatness. America is called the Great Experiment for good reason. We are free to test boundaries. The freer our economics the more confidence we have in executing our ideas. The broader our set of ideas coupled with the more open our options for investment, the more likely consumers will get an increased number of competitive products to choose from.

When our political, economic, social and cultural freedoms are restricted by government, our confidence wanes. Whether through government monopolies, or the political monopoly established by Democrats and Republicans, without the catalyst of freedom, the competitive, chemical reaction for success is crushed.

Conclusions

The Capitalist approach requires simple, smart rules for the competition. This is no easy task, but the ultimate requirement is for good governance. Equality is no easy task either in that it requires law that absolutely assures equal outcomes, which diminishes our freedoms. The Soviet Union had very equal outcomes, but their ultimate demise occurred when the government, as Margaret Thatcher put it, ran out of 'people's money.' Equality is important, especially for our criminal laws, but our freedoms must be preeminent if we are to succeed as a nation.

TWO-CLASS SOCIETY
VERSUS FLUID SOCIETIES

"If you want to see the true measure of a man,
watch how he treats his inferiors, not his equals."
J. K. Rowling

MARX HOPED TO CREATE A classless society, believing that Capitalism alienated the worker from their labor and their humanity. Marx also believed Capitalism also separated the worker, the proletariat, from *quality* leadership. Leaders of business, the bourgeoisie, were after profits—not worker satisfaction.

Bourgeoisie roughly translates to middle class and the nouveau rich that had flourished during the Renaissance and Industrial Revolution. As many of the bourgeoisie successfully launched businesses that created great wealth, it is easily assumed that Marx's class complaint also extended to the rich and the exceptionally rich which included the nobility and the church. The proletariat was further displaced from personal success due to the alienation of his/her labor by the emerging industrial mechanization of manufacturing processes. Marx may be correct, by degree, about alienation. A factory worker whose job was a cog in the division of labor along the manufacturing line may have not felt the same way as a master craftsman who designed, styled and built the entire product. Is there alienation? Perhaps, but not enough to mitigate movement of workers from farms they rented from the nobility—where they barely achieved subsistence—to industrial jobs in the cities that produced real pay in schillings and pounds. Alienation be damned as the money was better in the cities.

Marx, however, was clear that the proletariat and bourgeoisie were not competing for who would run the government. In fact, there was no competition. The leaders would be self-appointed superiors.

The bourgeoisie, wherever it has got the upper hand, has put an end to
all feudal, patriarchal, idyllic relations. It has pitilessly torn asunder the
motley feudal ties that bound man to his "natural superiors," and has

left remaining no other nexus between man and man than naked self-interest, than callous "cash payment." (More on about 'cash payment' in the next section.)

Idyllic relations of feudal times? Really. Marx saw the former feudal structure where citizens uniformly worked land for sustenance as the ideal. His central challenge, though, was who was in charge, the nobility in feudal times or dictators in Marx's Socialist regime.

Who are Marx's *natural superiors*? The revolutionaries, whoever they may be, especially intellectual revolutionaries and the politically astute and right minded. During the French Revolution in 1789, the Reign of Terror leaders were the revolutionaries behind the barricades. The guillotine was the preferred method of reeducating the former, tenured leadership. In the twenty-first century, Russia and China used other methods—gulags and cultural war gangs—to purge the old and usher in the new, which were equally as violent as the guillotine. Concerning Marx's new leaders—only the revolutionary intelligentsia should apply for the role of *natural superiors*.

Though Marx proposed the eradication of the bourgeoisie in the new world order, in the world order of his time, at the height of the industrial revolution, he lauded their energy to remake an extremely poor, feudal Europe into something quite spectacular. It seemed he had a love-hate relationship regarding Capitalism. Quoting from the *Communist Manifesto*:

The bourgeoisie, during its rule of scarce one hundred years, has created more massive and more colossal productive forces than have all preceding generations together. Subjection of Nature's forces to man, machinery, application of chemistry to industry and agriculture, steam-navigation, railways, electric telegraphs, clearing of whole continents for cultivation, canalisation of rivers, whole populations conjured out of the ground--what earlier century had even a presentiment that such productive forces slumbered in the lap of social labour? (Karl Marx, 1848) Marx, Karl; Engels, Friedrich. The Communist Manifesto (p. 5). Public Domain Books. Kindle Edition.

Many citizens who migrated from rural agricultural work took jobs as industrial workers in growing urban areas. Many created businesses. These bourgeoisie became the uncommon commoners, the ingenious commoners, the evolving *nouveau riche*, an upwardly mobile class that anyone could join. There were no class distinctions for entry into this club. One's position in the economy was determined by one's industriousness and creativity which had no limits. Even in the mid-eighteenth century, the movement between classes had begun to net amazing results.

Rapid industrialization, though, produced a very dingy and dirty environment in London where Marx lived. It is understandable that his view of the industrial revolution reflected the social and economic challenges to the worker. Marx's theory and its execution, however, did not improve the proletariat economic position; it created two classes: One included the proletariat, bourgeoisie, the rich and the nobility, and the second class was leadership, a special group of its own making.

Escaping Marx's perspective was the fact that evolution of property rights and 'cash payment' were erasing the lines between classes. These evolving freedoms motivated persons that would take a risk to execute a new idea, a new business. If personal success and industry could create a solid income or a grand income that created wealth, economic mobility then stirred more success and fewer class distinctions. In nations like Industrial England, much of Europe, and the United States, where land was relatively free and universally available, one's place in society was determined largely by one's labor, which per Locke, was owned by the individual, and unlike Marx, not alienating in any way. For Marx, by abolishing property, he abolished one's rights, one's freedom to own his own body and labor. His *natural superiors*, however, would own *him* lock, stock and barrel.

Capitalist societies are not a classless society so much as they are a culture where economic position is not designated government, nor by kings, queens, and popes, nor Marx's elites, experts, and secular theists, but by the individual. Capitalism creates a fluid economic system, where no one position is predetermined by class. The fewer guardrails that hem in the individual, the more likely the individual will rise to the highest level his 'self-interest' allows or desires. Capitalism creates a flowing and flexible society with citizens moving up *and down* the economic, social and cultural ladder dependent only on the willingness to work and increase their human capital. Five percent of America's least financially capable rise to the highest income class during their work lives. At the top, millionaires come and go, and wealth created by one generation is, more likely than not, lost in the next generation.

The harshness of feudal governance and Marx's Socialism is marked by the striking similarity of who determines one's destiny—their natural superiors or unnatural nobility. Democratic Capitalism assures that the individual oversees their destiny. For feudalism, Socialism and tyranny, one's position in life is determined by the State with little flexibility given to the individual.

Feudal lords administered serfs' lives and livelihoods. Democratic Socialist engineers dictate the rules of conduct for citizens of their perfect society. Tyrants are all about selfish interest (not self-interest) and they spend political energy assuring that citizens do not threaten their fiefdom.

More Marx

For Rousseau, land belonged to no one. For Marx, property belonged to everyone, which meant no one but the State. In the USSR, labor was not alienated because everyone made close to the same amount of money and worked for the *glorious state. "From each according to his ability, to each according to his needs!"* stated Marx. One's labor was owned by the state (natural leader) and the State did not much care about alienation. The Dictatorship of the Proletariat was not a one-time paradigm shift; it was a permanent political harness—that is a one-size-fits-all dictatorship—forever. In a perfect Socialist world, as man is perfected by the Dictatorship of the Proletariat, government need not transcend to the Socialist paradigm; the autocratic government is the paradigm. The perfect man never arrived by Communist standards, so the Dictatorship was always extended to the next five-year plan. Some political organizing structure was always needed to coordinate society in civil and sensible practices. For Marx, it was the Dictatorship of the Proletariat. For today's Socialist approach, it is an ever expanding, ever strengthening central government.

As thinking evolved about Socialism, and as science answered more and more questions about the universe and our daily lives, Scientific Socialism found a haven in Socialist marketing.

Today, Americans hear from the Left, and on occasion from Conservatives, about their love for science. Hilary Clinton, in her DNC acceptance speech in 2016 said, "I love science." Probably not. Few politicians or voters spend any time trying to educate themselves about science. During the COVID outbreak, the Left could not say often enough that they would follow the science. Few did, but saying they were on the side of science provided political cover and good personal branding. Sadly, for most purveyors of the love of science, none educated us on the details of their love or the science. As each nation around the world deployed a slightly different 'scientific approach' to mitigating COVID, no clear winner emerged, which is probably a good thing, because there is not likely to be a single policy that would work effectively in all situations.

John Kerry, during his presidential run in 2004, noted during a Senate climate meeting that "Science is Science." This is a beautiful tautology with zero meaning. He wanted to align his brand with science. He wanted to be the scientific Socialist promoting a single remedy for reducing carbon dioxide and saving the world. He applied his comment to endorse that the very new science of climate was complete and that he had the singular answer. He grasped the problem, and he had *the* answer, the scientific answer, the only answer, so climate science was complete and final. The science was done. Except that it was not true. Climate modeling is both interesting and valuable, but, as the aphorism in the scientific community goes, *models are always wrong but helpful*. As noted earlier, science begins its evolutionary ride when models turn into equations that can be validated. As recently noted by climate scientist, Bjorn Lomborg, the net impact of the Paris Climate protocols and the recently released Biden proposal on temperature by the end of the century, with expected spending near $80 trillion, is 0.2 degrees. With Mr. Kerry now the lead for the Biden climate proposition, whether the science surrounding the numerous climate models has been well transmitted to the media and the pols, should make citizens wonder if the medicine cures the patient.

In *Unsettled,* Dr Steven E. Koonin, President Obama's Science Advisor for the Department of Energy, delineates the challenges of acquiring scientific information from the layers of communications from climate data in the UN's IPCC reports, through summaries provided by independent organizations, through politicians then the media:

Today, the shift toward the alarming – and shareable – has traveled well beyond the headlines. That's especially true in climate and energy matters.

Whatever its noble intentions, news is ultimately a business, on that in this digital era increasingly depends on eyeballs in the form of click and shares. Reporting on the scientific reality that there's been hardly any long-term change in extreme weather doesn't fit the ethos of If it bleeds it leads.

Koonin is not a Conservative denier. As an Obama advocate, though, he is begging for rationality in scientific discovery and science reporting. His urgent request is as a centrist scientist begging for a return to the Baconian Scientific Method starting with the data and testing all the way through the communications process which ends with the citizen reading a news report. Put simply, that means less alarmist reporting, more reasonable exploration and validation of the data. And climate reporting isn't our only challenge. Koonin quotes H. L Mencken's *In Defense of Women*: *"The whole aim of practical politics is to keep the populace alarmed (and hence clamorous to be led to safety) by menacing it with an endless series of hobgoblins, most of the imaginary."* Though the quote is from 1918, it is a perfect fit for this century.

Washington wonks across both parties have continued to restate their *science,* and not just concerning climate but any political endeavor, with continued emphasis that if there are answers at all, that, more likely than not, answers will lie with experts in Washington, not among the commoners.

Americans have come to believe this 'Washington has the answer' conception of governance, something that would have seemed a bit insane only sixty years ago, is possible and desired and reasonable. In *Ideas Having Sex with Ideas (by this author),* a look back to the 1950s gives insight about the changes in American attitude about governance:

Over the last one hundred years the escalating interventions by government in our lives has led to the misconception that government could solve our problems. Yet, after decades of low performance and swelling distrust of government, now at 80 percent, Americans too often believe 'there oughta be law' or a program or spending or some intervention. After so much failure and mediocrity, why do Americans believe the government still needs to stick its nose in our business? Good question. Given the amount of money spent each election on telling Americans government can fix just about anything, and given our short memories, maybe the disconnect is not unreasonable.

Not so long ago, however, during the 1950s, when trust in government approached 80 percent, citizens understood that politicians were not miracle workers, they were people just like us. As art mimics life, a dinner conversation in a great science fiction film, 'The Day the Earth Stood Still,' provides great insight to the view of government at the time. The conversation turned to how the government could him find the film's star, Michael Rennie, the starman (he and Gort had recently land in the Capitol Mall from outer space) the government sought, who was sitting at the dinner table at a lodging house discussing ... him. No one at the table knew he was the starman. When the topic came up about government help, a young man responded that he was skeptical the government could help because the people in the government were just like us regular folks. Another dinner guest suggested that the government wasn't just like us, 'they're Democrats,' which is a bit ironic considering today's Democrats tilt toward scientific socialism where government purports to be an expert as everything.

The left's current obsession as government as expert at everything has produced results that suggests the opposite. To repeat, eighty percent of us do not trust government and so the 'oughta be a law' response seems counter-intuitive. Why give government more power when it hasn't done well in most of its previous endeavors? Why? The billions of dollars spent each election cycle tells us that the government is the answer, and the more political, complex, confusing and expensive the better.

America is at loggerheads with itself. As our *natural leaders*, our government, has grown in breadth and depth, our trust in government has dropped precipitously to under 20 percent, mostly because our leaders have not produced great or even good results. Yet citizens are more and more likely to desire a government that not only engineers solutions; citizens command responsibility for operational execution of social monopolies which government routinely does poorly—reducing our trust more. This trust death-spiral has been devolving for one hundred years. It is the Socialist approach, with science as the stated engineer, that tells us, "We have the answer" and then the answer is problematic and resultless. The Scientific Socialist approach, though, that, *"We are here for the federal government and here to help"* just sounds so good it must be true. Why? Because we keep buying into the warm blanket political marketing and continue to cast our votes for it. Though it does not take long to discover the proposition sounded better than the execution, we keep voting for the clever marketing despite the lack of execution and results. Good marketing beats reality every day. The poor results, however, are about to take their toll on our children and the minority citizens that have been very poorly served by big Socialist monopolies.

More about Capitalism and property from Schumpeter.

The task of piecing together such fragments is delicate and cannot be attempted here. The basic idea is clear enough, however. The stratifying principle consists in the ownership, or the exclusion from ownership, of means of production such as factory buildings, machinery, raw materials and the consumers' goods that enter into the workman's budget. We have thus, fundamentally, two and only two classes, those owners, the capitalists, and those have-nots who are compelled to sell their labor, the laboring class or proletariat. The existence of intermediate groups, such as are formed by farmers or artisans who employ labor but also do manual work, by clerks and by the professions is of course not denied; but they are treated as anomalies which tend to disappear in the course of the capitalist process. The two fundamental classes are, by virtue of the logic of their position and quite independently of any individual volition, essentially antagonistic to each other. Rifts within each class and collisions between subgroups occur and may even have historically decisive importance. But in the last analysis, such rifts or collisions are incidental. The one antagonism that is not incidental but inherent in the basic design of capitalist society is founded upon the private control over the means to produce: the very nature of the relation between the capitalist class and the proletariat is strife—class war. Schumpeter, Joseph. Capitalism, Socialism, and Democracy (Kindle Locations 357-367). Start Publishing LLC. Kindle Edition.

And...

On the other hand, Marx wished to define capitalism by the same trait that also defines his class division. A little reflection will convince the reader that this is not a necessary or natural thing to do. In fact, it was a bold stroke of analytic strategy which linked the fate of the class phenomenon with the fate of capitalism in such a way that socialism, which in reality has nothing to do with the presence or absence of social classes, became, by definition, the only possible kind of classless society, excepting primitive groups. This ingenious tautology could not equally well have been secured by any definitions of classes and of capitalism other than those chosen by Marx—the definition by private ownership of means of production. Hence there had to be just two classes, owners and non-owners, and hence all other principles of division, much more plausible ones among them, had to be severely neglected or discounted or else reduced to that one. Schumpeter, Joseph. Capitalism, Socialism, and Democracy (Kindle Locations 443-450). Start Publishing LLC. Kindle Edition.

The division of classes into owners and non-owners is interesting and a somewhat accurate description of mid-eighteenth-century London. The division between owners and non-owners is an accurate rendering of Marx's thinking as well as today's Leftist belief system. Marx's rendering of the world—lots of workers and those damnable business owners, the bourgeoisie, were creating a mess, as previously noted. *London was no Nirvana*. Marx, though, puts both groups into a single class, and then creates a new class, the overlords, creating a two-class society. His classless, two-class society is based on a misunderstanding of owners and non-owners in a Capitalist society that proposes these groups are static. Marx missed the fact that membership of these groups changed over time. Individuals changed, evolved. The group's memberships cross pollinated. Even during the very squalid times during the English Industrial Revolution, in the very dirty city of London, the owners and non-owners were not locked groups. Income mobility meant persons rose and fell from one group to the other, perpetually.

Most American families are probably much like my own whose grandparents were poor farmers. My grandparents' offspring produced one professional and one owner, neither wealthy but vastly better off than my grandparents, and the next generation produced a handful of middle-class workers, a couple of upper middle-class professionals, and two very wealthy owners, most of whom were first-generation college graduates. It is very possible the next generation will produce a new mix of classes with some doing very well, some doing average and a few that have economic challenges.

A fluid society is attainable and has been in play for a few centuries. A classless society is just homogenized income levels that deaden any otherwise thriving economy and always devolve into two classes: the commoners and the natural superiors. Since classes are free and fluid in a Capitalist society, and individuals may traverse many income quintiles during their work life, income inequality is much less important than income mobility, wealth inequality, and one's human Capitalism quotient. More on income inequality under the heading *Social Justice Versus Individual Justice*.

Elites and Democratic Capitalists and Socialists

Though Socialism devolves to a two-class society, the same devolution can, and has, occurred in Capitalist democracies, via the politics of the Left and with complicity from Conservatives. America is a good example of both Socialists and Capitalists using their economic might and intellectual girth to create a class of elites that run our government. In the last election $14 billion dollars were spent on political campaigns, the large majority of which came from big donations by big business, big unions, highly paid intellectual elites, and rich special interests. Another $3 billion was expended for lobbying Congress, funded by the same groups.

In 2016, Hillary Clinton captured the thinking of elites about the rest of America with her comment about Trump supporters being a 'basket of deplorables.' Elites on the Conservative side of the aisle think in parallel terms. Is this crazy? Take a vacation in Washington and try making an appointment to talk to your Congressman, a DC reporter or someone from a think tank. Unless you're a somebody, even if requesting an appointment to discuss the best idea since sliced bread, your request will go into a black hole. If you write a $2,500 check, you might get a short meeting. Maybe.

Politics is a market, a market of elites. The political parties have erected a duopoly which owns the voting supply chain, the big money that supplies revenue to run the organizations, and the legislative authority to create rules which create substantial barriers to hobble political entrepreneurs. They have effectively stunted any innovation that would help our nation run smarter, run better and run more effectively.

Conclusions

Though the two-party system has served America well, we may have the wrong two political parties to help serve Americans' twenty-first century interests. These two aging monopolistic institutions are like dinosaurs stacked high with money bags leading us to the tarpits. The worst of this arrangement, though, is that the political monopoly created by Democrats and Republicans has morphed into a new class of elites. Two other classes exist: the commoners and the class of Forgotten Men (and Women).

In what should be a fluid society for all members, each group's membership appears to be solidifying. Economic mobility has declined over the last decades as the public has consistently not delivered a quality education to poor and rural students. In *Coming Apart: America's New Cultural Divide*, Charles Murray provides astonishing detail about the separation of income groups from poor to rich and the debilitating effects on the pursuit of the poor to attain happiness and economic success. During the mid-twentieth century, classes mixed in education and in marriage and raised all boats. The classes are now diverging in Murray's fictional cities of Fishtown and Belmont, a perfect picture of American society. These onerous divides are in large part created by government assistance programs that provide reparations for the government's inability to provide the single essential blocking block to a better life: an education.

In an age of innovation, our government needs to foster innovation in the marketplace but also to foster innovation in government and politics. Opening political markets would help, but the likelihood of the political parties ushering competition for new parties is outside the realm of possibility. Our would-be kings and queens are as unlikely to give up their thrones as Crazy King George is likely to give up his crown. Only the voter can decide that in the age of the lumbering dinosaurs the voter needs some competition.

The voters have shown their displeasure for elites and their 'down the nose' view of Americans. Donald Trump, despite all his warts and in part because of all his warts, won the 2016 election against all possible odds. Had he more comity, he may have won in 2020. Joe Biden was elected both because of Trump's warts and Biden's billions in donations from the extraordinarily rich and the marketing of a unity message. The parties remained well aligned with their fully diverging political platforms, one to the Left and one Conservative, driven by aging status quo platforms, with no new ideas that were not a rehash of ideas already proposed and failed in previous administrations. In other words, America has not moved ahead; it simply changed leaders. Culturally, politically and economically, we would have to speed up just to stop. America is flopping back and forth between two sets of elites without a plan for American excellence that will compete with China's avowed mission to sideline our leadership.

A little fluidity is needed not just in our economy, but in politics too. The voters need an open market where they are free to vote for a variety of products. Until then, we are struck in a three-class society, the forgotten, the great middle, and the elites.

The elites will continue to offer experts as evidence of the divine right of leadership, which like scientific marketing may not be all we would hope for.

MICROMANAGEMENT VERSUS ENLIGHTENED LEADERSHIP

HAVING DISCUSSED OPTIMISM/PESSIMISM, TRUST/DISTRUST, SELF- and selfish-interest, there is both a personal as well as an ideological variable to consider for each. To be clear, as people, not all Capitalists are optimistic; some are pessimists. Not all Socialists lack trust in their fellow man. As ideologies, however, the predisposition of the ideologies differ from personal habits. The propensities of policy created by Socialist experts often crater because of their lack of trust in the individual, whether worker or owner. Capitalist competition and open markets are optimistic about consumer outcomes if only because millions of consumers seldom buy a poor product twice. Bad businesses with bad leaders fail. And so it is with micromanagement versus enlightened leadership. Each suffers the same personal versus public policy dichotomy. An individual Capitalist may be as fierce a micromanager as a government regulatory agency lording over national policy. More troubling is the fact that few leaders are multipliers of ideas in business or government. Given this, the mission is exploring how Socialism and Capitalism, as ideologies, align with more restrictive versus less restrictive leadership, not personal traits.

Imagine this. While seeking employment, you are able to schedule two job interviews for a sales position. Suited up for the first interview, the VP of Sales arrives with a 2,000-page tome and says, "Our company went through a downsizing because of the recent recession. To recover we completely rewrote our sales plan down to the finest detail, reduced the size of our engineering group, but increased the number of products. This manual is an unbelievably detailed overview of all products and our extensive sales process so there no questions for the salesperson about how to sell each product."

He flops the manual on the table for your perusal. "Any question the customer may ask, the answer is in here. There are twenty-three widgets we sell where we previously had only ten. We believe more widgets the better. If you get the job, over the first two weeks you will need to familiarize yourself with the details of the manual and be able to execute the process flawlessly. The annual quota is X and the pay for reaching the quote is Y dollars. Not making quota means probation, evaluated monthly. No additional pay will be paid for selling beyond quota. Your sales manager will review your work ethic hourly and listen to calls regularly to make sure you are following the process. Weekly performance reviews are on Friday afternoons at five o'clock. Commissions for sales will not be paid until you make quota for the year."

For anyone who has trained for a new job, a 2,000-page manual is staggering. That someone is listening over your shoulder to make sure you are doing your job is not one bit pleasant for anyone. Weekly reviews are too much management for anyone to endure. The detailed manual, all 2,000 pages, is not likely to be an educational security blanket, but a staggeringly complex document that will make it impossible for the salesperson to stay inside the innumerable strictures. This is too much information to understand.

For those readers who have not worked in sales, the incentive to be a salesperson is to overachieve quota and make additional money. For the hourly worker, exceeding quota is much like overtime at time and a half. If the hourly worker were asked to work overtime for no pay, that dog won't hunt. That you wouldn't get paid commissions for sales until you hit 100 percent of your target is another red flag. Few would take the job.

As important, most of us would gag having to work in a business with a manager lurking behind the chair, watching your every move.

This is how the Socialist approach to government works. Obamacare is a great example. Its 2,000-page executive summary passed by Congress morphed into another 18,000 pages of detailed regulation about how the nuts and bolts of the program *should* work, including the 150+ committees invented to assure the government could appropriately restrict pricing; how insurance companies would conform to process; and how the fifty million people without insurance should act including a mandate to buy insurance. The program did not fail to reduce the cost of insurance so much because of lack of good intentions as it failed under the weight of its own complexity and distrust of its bureaucrats, the insurance companies, and the consumer. Obamacare, like the complex sales process, is micromanagement at its worst and is seldom, if ever, successful.

The second interview is quite different.

The vice president of sales states, "Our company went through a down-sizing because of the recent recession. To recover we completely rewrote the sales plan to simplify the product set and the sales process. The process is six easy steps for the salesperson to walk through with the customer—to qualify their need, find a good fit for the solution, demonstrate the product, price it correctly and ask for the business. Reducing the number of products and therefore being able to spend more time and money on improved quality we believe will assure more business, but also more repeat business. The quota is an annual quota but broken out into monthly chunks with commissions paid monthly. You get paid a commission on every sale including the first one, and exceeding annual quota creates accelerators for commissions. We are looking for salespersons that want to exceed the expectations of our customers but also to exceed their own goals. There is plenty of room for people who also seek leadership positions as part of their roadmap for success."

Simplicity is the mother of success in process, in products and policy for business. Adding the freedom to excel also adds to a great work environment. Big companies can scale because they provide products, sometimes simple products like a smart phone and sometimes complex products like an air-liner, of value to the consumer. Big companies incent workers to align with company goals, which translates to pay for performance. People that perform well are retained and promoted. Those that do not perform well find new em-ployment. If the reader believes this sounds harsh, understand that being let go from a business is the way most workers remake themselves or seek a new profession, which is a good thing, not bad.

As micromanaged governance does not work well, nor do microman-aged businesses. They tend not to scale well and tend to top out when the leaders are overwhelmed by their constant need to be involved in every de-cision and transaction. Despite the inefficiency of micro-management, even the best managed businesses employ micromanagers who gum up what should be a successful pipeline of talented employees. In larger companies, micromanagers are discovered when turnover in their department is high because people leave for new jobs or because of high rates of firing.

I worked for a very highly regulated monopoly early in my career. Headquarters published and distributed a multi-volume, multi-thousand page, tome of rules, regulations, processes, and procedures for every conceivable situation. Though known to be one of the best run companies in the world, it was old, stodgy and its products were complex and expensive. Though known for innovation, innovations were about incremental changes to aging technology. The answer to whether a monopoly can work, and well, in the case of this company, the answer was yes, but the sell by date on its technology had expired. The company was a great example of government monopolies that can work, but the workability in a world of change compromised its long-term success. The monopoly was broken up in the 1980s as even Congress understood that the company had become a barrier to innovation in its industry.

Conclusion

The Socialist approach for federal policy is, by its very precepts, government by micromanagement. Experts are tapped to create some perfect set of detailed requirements to perfect how citizens engage is the very definition of micromanagement. Whether the prescriptive FDR programs like the National Industrial Recovery Act, or later additions from other administrations like Medicare, Obamacare, or our extensive 75,000-page IRS tax code, it seems to be a natural proclivity of the Socialist approach to finely detail rules and regulations.

Even in the business world is filled with multi-thousand-page manuals that fill our cubbies micromanagement is alive and well. The *PA Times* reports: "A survey conducted by Trinity Solutions and published in author Harry Chambers' book *My Way or the Highway* showed that 79 percent of respondents had experienced micromanagement. Approximately 69 percent said they considered changing jobs because of micromanagement and another 36 percent changed jobs. Seventy-one percent said being micromanaged interfered with their job performance while 85 percent said their morale was negatively impacted." Not pretty. We are human after all, and sometimes not in a good way. As there is no school that teaches the basic principles of leadership and so few opportunities to learn how to lead as we grow up, too often the default is to be the manager looking over one's shoulder.

Having a micromanaging manager is one thing. Having a government based on micromanaging our conduct down to the finest detail, is quite another problem.

Great leaders, business or political, are multipliers. They ask for input. They solicit ideas. They provide straightforward guidance. Poor leaders hope to control conduct, and this is the challenge of the Socialist approach. The conceit that a perfect approach to our lives is known by the controller/expert who can extensively detail government policy and business conduct, is the first step in assuring poor governance. It is also the first step in the ever-increasing complexity of our government.

It's not hard to see the micromanagement of the Socialist approach, especially this century. The Left has increased our regulatory environment, while Conservatives thin regulations. This was not always the case. Bill Clinton stated flatly during the 1996 State of the Union Address, that "the era of big government is over." In fact, Clinton and Gore teamed up to streamline regulations, programs and policies to the point that the cost of government (remember this is overhead, our nation's SGA expense) totaled 17.44 percent (according to the Fed) of GDP by the end of his tenure, the lowest in decades. The pre-COVID numbers in 2019 has risen to 21.74. That's a 21 percent increase in the cost of America doing business. This doesn't include the nearly $2 trillion in regulatory compliance costs.

The question for the reader: Are the extra costs improving Americans' lives? Secondarily, do we really need a government that is looking over our shoulders or providing products that we can acquire privately, without much or only simple government oversight?

Who wins this round comes down to this: What type of leader do you want? A more effective government, however, one with lower overhead costs that the citizen must bear in regulation and taxes, is a government that is simpler, smarter and more trusting of its citizens.

EXPERTS VERSUS THE EVOLUTION OF IDEAS

"Every man gets a narrower and narrower field of knowledge in which he must be an expert in order to compete with other people. The specialist knows more and more about less and less and finally knows everything about nothing."
Konrad Lorenz

MOST OF US ARE LIKELY to whip out our phones when looking for information—the response arrives in milliseconds. We've been conditioned to believe ready answers are available for everything with a swipe of our fingers Do you want to know 2020 Q4 GDP was? Siri says, "4.1 percent." The answer highlighted at the top of the page, published as a fact, and it is, followed by 14.7 million other responses which none of us look at. No stretch of the imagination is required to take an intellectual leap from our quick access to information on Google to, "How do you build a financing system for the individual health insurance market." This question produces 486 million listings; the first page highlights a variety of books and papers about how financing your health care has been provided over the last many decades. The authors are experts or tout themselves as such. Without checking credentials, these experts are surely well educated and well read. If you want an answer to fact-based questions, the Internet is your friend. Regarding health care financing, the variety of possible answers is vast, each from an expert, all differing in content and construction. Facts are relatively easy to assess. Solutions never arrive in one-size-fits-all packaging.

We vote for politicians whom we hope will hire the best and brightest experts that can help guide our nation. Experts, though, are not the class of people we believe they are according to psychologist Phillip Tetlock, who worked for the Reagan administration, tasked with, "working out what the Soviet response might be to the Reagan's administration's hawkish stance in the Cold War." As he had no experience in international policy, his manager advised him to ask an expert for advice to shape policy. His investigation, however, produced reams of conflicting possibilities from a spectrum of experts. After he served Reagan, he delved deeper into the value of expert advice. He surveyed three hundred experts asking "specific, quantifiable forecasts—answering 27,450 of his question between them—and then waited to see whether their forecasts came true. They rarely did." (Harford, Adapt, 2011) Getting consensus from any group of experts is unlikely. Choosing what may be the best way forward from the fog of information is a crapshoot at best. More than likely, social and economic problems have an array of solutions that, if implemented, run the gamut of effectiveness from poor to very good.

Scientific Socialism's fundamental proposal is that experts can produce a single, perfected solution. This default leadership paradigm of Washington elites from both parties leaves American citizens to believe that simple answers are readily available from experts. Though this proposition was generally adopted by the Left, the approach leaks into conservative thinking as well. During the 2020, election, an unnamed congresswoman when asked about health care financing suggested that something could be whipped up, like it was no big deal. The voter tends to ride the wave of optimism about solutions being ready at hand if only because our default position is that we believe what they tell us is true. In *Talking to Strangers,* Malcolm Gladwell provides numerous examples of how we default to the truth when we listen to our friends, politicians, even strangers. We want to believe what we hear if only because the information providers in media and from politicians seems to be delivered with honest intent. The confidence when providing a grand message that a solution is just a conversation (or two away) diverges when outcomes of policy are tracked and measured. Can a group of experts come up with a simple solution that both provides great health care and reduced costs? That was the impression given by the congresswoman. As Tetlock discovered when asking experts, numerous answers followed, and few predictions came true.

There are no experts. Our belief in an expert-run Washington is based on intellectual conceit, not reality. There are, however, a broad range of well-educated wonks with opinions and many are of dubious quality. Sorting out what is a good idea never occurs. Aging partisan proposals that fit the political paradigm are shoe-horned into policy. Once immortalized in law, outcomes become less important than political will and power.

On the market side, entrepreneurs, America's commercial problem-solvers, are not experts so much as they are emerging experts. Ask a broad group of entrepreneurs to invent a new widget and the number of new designs will equal the number of entrepreneurs. This competing community of experts understands that the ultimate arbiter of their new ideas is the consumer. They are not successful experts until the consumer decides. No one asks entrepreneurs to devise new products, because they are already in the process of creation, all the time, nonstop, on one project or another, until they find success in the marketplace, which is the difference between experts and entrepreneurs. Experts have knowledge of the past and how problems were solved. In as much as entrepreneurs do not necessarily agree with one another, they do not focus on past solutions, the status quo, but the needs of the potential of innovation. Entrepreneurs look forward and solve tomorrow's problems today.

Political experts do not act like entrepreneurs; nor do the persons who engage them for their knowledge. They are not much worried about success but about applying formerly used—and seldom effective solutions—to build policy. Because much of government is ineffective—either from lack of social results or poor financial sustainability—ideas formulated using old, poorly performing mechanisms do not move America's needle of success.

Government policy is not scientific, not in any way. It is not evidence based. It is guesswork where administrators get caught in complex bureaucratic machinery that is not flexible nor responsive to change. Worse, policies are implemented without an iota of testing. Elites believe they are so special that their ideas do not need testing. Their conceit is shocking.

Though the expert mentality is most assuredly a result of both citizens and leaders believing that big national programs must have readily available answers, both Socialist and Capitalist approaches to our Democracy have been co-opted by expert governance where most experts believe their ideas are infallible (i.e., they are a religious offshoot of the pope) and yet few experts agree on anything. Worse, because government tends to create solutions that are fixed in time, immortal, this senescent approach is not a good mix for the twenty-first century where exponential change is the rule, not the exception, and the rate of change is increasing.

No one should recommend excising the experts from government. Their education and their historical knowledge are important. The question, though, is how to make government and the policies and program created by experts more entrepreneurial, more testable, more flexible and more results oriented. We need a new kind of expert and a new type of leader. Our political parties, though, are mired in the status quo. Change, especially transformational change, is impossible, without new voices from new competing political parties.

Evolution of Ideas

As recommended earlier, though science is understood by most of us as a one-and-done endeavor, this view could not be further from the truth. Science is a continuous debate of proposed theories, where according to science historian and philosopher Karl Popper, well-designed methods are used to create data that supports a theory, or more importantly, falsifies the theory. Proposing a theory that cannot be falsified via testing will be little more than a theory or religion. From *Scientific American*, "While a pseudo-science is set up to look for evidence that supports its claims, science philosopher Karl Popper says, 'science is set up to challenge its claims and look for evidence that might prove it false.'"

While Popper and others note the challenges presented in the collection of data and assurance that the data is accurate, once data arrives for interpretation, science takes an edgy, wiggly turn. About one experimental theory, he illustrates, the challenges of mere humans endeavoring to discover both methods of science and their outputs: ". . . the postdoctoral fellows, the junior scientists, the quiet, decent majority flying in science's economy class – followed rules. Heedless official restrictions, they went on stuff the overhead bins of scientific inference with their moral, psychological, political and cultural baggage."

Science is extremely hard work if only because the challenges for obtaining quality data may take years, or decades, or centuries whereas scientists, despite the more psychological, political, and cultural baggage, have a universal respect for the data and the value of testing. Not unlike entrepreneurs, they are solving tomorrow's problems and waiting for the confirmation of other scientists to validate their ideas with more testing. Also, like entrepreneurs, their ideas succeed and live another day or are falsified and wind up like products that did not acquire consumers' stamp of approval.

The perceived context that an expert is someone in the know, like a scientist, is dubious at best. Our experts in Washington need to be much humbler about their abilities and the effectiveness of their theories which, many times, have been previously falsified by data or simply did not work as well as projected. Unfortunately, the competition among experts is more about spin that a universal respect for the data, the evidence, the validation of an idea.

Given the enormous challenges of scientific and entrepreneurial problem-solving, it is no wonder that politicians embrace the concept but run from its requirements.

Conclusions

There is a place for experts in government, just as there is room for experienced bureaucrats and politicians. What is absent is what scientists and entrepreneurs do. They experiment, test, analyze—over and over until something matches the hypothesis, and even then, the community of scientists tries to falsify the theory as well as promote a menu of other new ideas. In other words, our experts would benefit from much less conceit and much more humility in offering ideas for solutions regardless of which side of the political aisle one beckons from. Once an idea meets the math sniff test (do the data work) a test of the proposal to validate the solution is essential. If implemented, as the world is in constant change, the data needs to be constantly monitored and validated to assure the solutions continue to provide benefit and if it does not, changes must be made, or new solutions are investigated. Government that evolves is the only government which will be successful over long periods of time.

The Socialist, expert approach is not likely to embrace evidence-based government as it is not aligned with the land-expand-spend paradigm. Paradigms are not easily disrupted even for scientists. The Capitalists should love this approach, but one good option—the states as test beds—gets little traction in policy and less reporting by the press.

SELF-INTEREST, SELFISH INTEREST

*"The new world economic order is not an
exercise in philanthropy, but in enlightened
self-interest for everyone concerned."*
Carlos Fuentes

*"Wisdom ceases to be wisdom when it becomes
too proud to weep, too grave to laugh, and
too selfish to seek other than itself."*
Khalil Gibran

MARX'S DEROGATION OF ADAM'S SMITH narrative concerning self-interest morphed into a narrative about selfish interest which is not what Smith had in mind. In the *Theory of Moral Sentiments,* Smith writes:

How selfish soever man may be supposed, there are evidently some principles in his nature, which interest him in the fortune of others, and render their happiness necessary to him, though he derives nothing from it, except the pleasure of seeing it.) The Theory Of Moral Sentiments, Part I, Section I, Chapter I, p. 9, para.1.)

Some principles in his nature, which interest him in the fortune of others is *self-interest* which is a far cry from selfish interest. Self-interest attempts to understand one's life by accommodating the needs of others. Selfish interest has a singular objective, the needs of oneself, alone. Me first, the fortune of others later.

Smith expands with an example:

Whoever offers to another a bargain of any kind, proposes to do this. Give me that which I want, and you shall have this which you want, is the meaning of every such offer; and it is in this manner that we obtain from one another the far greater part of those good offices which we stand in need of. It is not from the benevolence of the butcher, the brewer, or the baker that we expect our dinner, but from their regard to their own interest. We address ourselves, not to their humanity, but to their self-love, and never talk to them of our own necessities, but of their advantages. (Smith, Adam. An Inquiry into the Nature and Causes of the Wealth of Nations (p. 10). University of Chicago Press. Kindle Edition.)

Smith's writing pre-dated Marx's by less than a century. Both lived in Great Britain. Marx's London was three times bigger than London when Smith attended Oxford. Both saw the harsh effects of the Industrial Revolution. Each, though, drew vastly different and divergent conclusions about mankind. Both are accurate. There isn't an off/on switch for the effects of industrialization that measures good and bad. Both Marx and Smith can be correct without presuming the other wrong.

There are owners, like Smith's butcher, that hope to assure there is a quality exchange of goods that benefits both the buyer and the butcher. Why? Because the butcher wants the consumer as a return customer, today, tomorrow and throughout the future.

Are there proletarians who have been taken advantage of by owners seeking only to maximize their profits to the exclusion of their workers' or customers' benefit. Absolutely. Marx's view is of an ugly present that will not correctly evolve in the future without the very visible and heavy hand of government. In reality, businesses that only work in terms of self-interest have a very short shelf life because the value of the products they sell declines in quality and increases in price. More simply—selfishness, if it works at all, works only for short periods.

The question to the reader: Is humanity generally described by Smith's self-interest or in the need of Marx's Dictatorship of the Proletariat to remedy man's selfishness, among other human deficiencies.

More Smith: how self-interest integrates into our need to improve our lives.

The natural effort of every individual to better his own condition, when suffered to exert itself with freedom and security, is so powerful a principle, that it is alone, and without any assistance, not only capable of carrying on the society to wealth and prosperity, but of surmounting a hundred impertinent obstructions, with which the folly of human laws too often encumbers its operations: though the effect of those obstructions is always, more or less, either to encroach upon its freedom, or to diminish its security. In Great Britain industry is perfectly secure; and though it is far from being perfectly free, it is as free or freer than in any other part of Europe. Smith, Adam. An Inquiry into the Nature and Causes of the Wealth of Nations (pp. 290-291). University of Chicago Press. Kindle Edition.

Extraordinarily few people have no interest in finding a path to improve their lives, to rise to the point of success that meets their needs. Whether owner or worker, we all hope to reach higher and to accomplish our goals via the accommodation of others, whether our bosses or our customers. We are *Social Animals* according to David Brooks. Is he correct? Or are we Socialist animals, according to Marx? We find new paths to raise our value personally (remember Alfred Marshall's survey) or to increase the value of our products and services to keep our customer coming back. If you are unsure that we are not in the game of improvement, consider that *if we were not*, we would still be living in a cave on a savannah.

Is there a small cohort of humans with no desire to perform well, to improve their condition? Absolutely. Are these groups the norm or the exception? People, after all, do act badly. We all do. We don't do it very often because there is no financial or social or personal payback for breaking laws or, for that matter, acting badly or selfishly. Worse, poor conduct over time advertises one's poor behavior and marginalizes that person with his peers. Governance based on a belief that we continuously act badly—and that a thick government playbook is required to keep us reigned in—seems to be the intention of Marx and today's democratic Socialists. Let's presume each of us is trying to improve every day and needs only simple guardrails to establish acceptable conduct. This presumption suggests that simpler governance is not only possible but should be the strategy.

Conclusion

Which society do we live in? One governed by self-interest in a relatively free society proposed by democratic Capitalism, or a society of the selfish, where selfish interest dominates and must be continually reined in by a strong, central, Socialist approach to government?

The answer may depend on whether the reader is an optimist or a pessimist.

PESSIMISM VERSUS OPTIMISM

To ASSURE A LEVEL LEXICAL playing field for readers, the definitions of these two words from online *Oxford Dictionary* are as follows:

Optimism: hopefulness and confidence about the future or the successful outcome of something. Synonyms: Similar: hopefulness, hope, confidence, sanguineness, positiveness. An example: the doctrine, especially as set forth by Leibniz, that this world is the best of all possible worlds.

Pessimism: a tendency to see the worst aspect of things or believe that the worst will happen; a lack of hope or confidence in the future. Synonyms: defeatism, negative thinking, expecting the worst, lack of hope, angst, distrust. An example: a belief that this world is as bad as it could be or that evil will ultimately prevail over good.

A voter or politician, regardless of political party affiliation, could be either an optimist or a pessimist. The nature of one's ideological approach to governance, however, assures a much higher propensity toward the results on governance being one or the other.

An optimist likely trends toward Adam Smith's thinking in the *Theory of Moral Sentiments*, that man generally tries to improve himself and without much help from government will find a road to some level of success while being accommodative to his fellow man. Optimism about an individual's journey is leveraged by a Ronald Reagan dictate: "Trust but verify." If it works, keep doing it. If it does not, do something different.

The pessimist among our human brethren may seek the weight of a strong central government as did Marx and his followers and many leaders in the western world's democracies, because the pessimist is more likely to see the bad in his peers and his situation and the need to lay out tight strictures to prevent bad behavior.

Marx's gloom about societies' selfishness created by Capitalism lends to directives that require the Socialist approach and some level of dictatorship or continual citizen reeducation to assure we are all in line according to central controllers. Many western governments around the world, including our own, assume that society is chock-full of persons with bad and selfish intentions who need to be controlled via law and regulation. In twenty-first-century America, re-education found an alternate challenge at our universities via safe spaces and the cancel culture.

Here's the rub with controllers. If society's perfection lay only at the feet of the strong, central government, then who controls the unlimited power of pessimistic *natural leaders?* Our leaders, like the rest of us, suffer the same Lockean challenge. Just as there is no divine right of kings, there is no secular right to membership in any set of *natural leaders.* They are self-appointed like the people behind the barricades in 1789 revolutionary France. The Socialist approach provides no guarantee that our leaders will be virtuous to lead the proletariat once they are installed. With absolute power, they succumb to the same corruption as kings, queens, and popes of yore. Even in America, where we elect our natural leaders, the intellectual and political corruption created by our government, a $4.8 trillion enterprise, the largest enterprise in the world, is gigantic. Our government is a massive, complex, confusing enterprise which is in the complete control of monied interests. Unsurprisingly, Gallup reports that 75 percent of Americans believe the federal government is corrupt. Though we live in a nation "of the people, by the people and for the people," our government is a runaway train going off an operational and financial cliff. Our politicians and elites invest heavily to enrich their treasures, whether ideologically or financially. Whether for dollars or dogma, pessimistic leadership assumes we need our kings and queens and elites to put us in line, instead of giving the freedom to individuals to act as a collection of wise citizens that produce a highly productive economy, society, and culture.

Optimism about mankind produces a style of governance that presumes that we all have personal and/or corporate challenges. Collectively, we understand there are bad players among us to navigate around, but that we are all deferential to good conduct, harsh about bad conduct, restrained in process, and directed by results. In Alexis de Tocqueville's book, *Democracy in America*, he wrote that as Americans migrated west, small settlements self-organized. When crime increased, a sheriff was sought. When conflicts arose, mayors and judges were sought. To this day, when problems arise, citizens engage to find solutions. At the personal level, we do the same. When friends and family have challenges, we help, if only to provide consolation. We make each other better by our very presence. Our self-interest incents our commiseration and our problem-solving. Our charity is essential to social health. Harry Truman saw our charity as something quite different. A longtime supporter of socialized medicine, he supported LBJ's announcement of Medicare in 1966 by commenting that it would be rid of the "indignity of charity." Our charity, whether in dollars or in personal support of our friends and family, is most essential human dignity and an essential characteristic of Americans as a collection of persons, not a collective. That our self-interest ushers in the best of our humanity, to help others, personally, is optimistic. No law is required.

The readers might ask what kind of person they are, an optimist or pessimist; what type of person for which they wish to work; and what type of leader they seek. Most of us identify as optimists, and even in an extremely challenging 2020, over half were optimistic about the future. On the other hand, regarding work, 76 percent believe we work for a micromanager which creates a toxic work environment. In choosing our political leaders, our optimism drops, not so much because we seek to vote for more laws and regulations and micromanagement, but because we have less trust in our fellow political man when they are looking over our shoulder. We may not need nor desire micromanagement, but that guy that lives down the from us? He's a mess. We need a law to reel him/her in. And that guy down the street, is probably looking back up the street and thinking the same thing. This makes for very effective political marketing, as that guy down the street can be a shill to engage both pessimists and optimists.

Pew Research has polled our level of trust for the last sixty years. While our trust in government has fallen from 80 percent *trusting* to 80% distrusting government, our trust in one another has also declined. We have become more pessimistic. Whether the culture of politics caused the drop in personal trust or vice versa is unclear, but distrust increases pessimism and diminishes our potential for success because those making laws and regulations will consistency see any single bad player or event as a giant wave preceding a bigger problem.

Perfectibility and Pessimism

The intersection of the utopian designs and Christian thinking during the late 19th century is still with us today in western governance. The common thread between religious and secular thinking is that individuals may have their moments of perfection – like a perfect score on a math test or a set of books that balance at the end of an accounting period – but that man is not perfect, nor is mankind, nor society, nor much of anything, which seems accurate. Perfection measured at any point in time reveals our imperfections. The pessimist sees the world in the moment and attempts to right the rules for perfection. The optimist sees the trend over time, whether decades, centuries, or millennia, and leads according to the trend. in *Enlightenment Now,* author Stephen Pinker writes about numerous human challenges from wealth, inequality, the environment, safety, health, democracy and fifteen other issues have over the last several centuries each improved markedly. That we have become more enlightened is a result of increasing political and economic freedoms. Our trend is not toward imperfection. Though imperfect, we are getting better. Armed with information like this, it is hard not to be optimistic. Is this information readily available from the press or media? Seldom! They are focused on events that paint the world on fire.

Christians believed man to be a sinner without much chance for personal recovery without God's guidance and forgiveness. The Utopians, unlike Christians, believed that the road to perfection was not through God but via perfect institutions or a perfect society that they wanted to engineer. This was Marx's approach.

The Capitalists, however, not religious nor social engineers, never presuming a perfect economy was possible outside textbooks, knew the world was messy, and that the possibility of a Capitalist economy working perfectly was zero. The perfect consumption of capital? Just a proposition never to occur. Perfect markets are possible but improbable because bad actors—individuals, institutions or the government—muck things up. A perfect price curve? The Phillips Curve? The effects of high public debt? The effects of tax cuts or tax increases? Most everything in economics, and in all social sciences for that matter, are probabilities and no economic process produced a 100 percent probability, that is perfection.

The difference between the optimism produced by the Capitalist approach and the pessimism of the Socialist lay with Adam's Smith butcher. When pricing his products for the customer, the process was continual, never quite perfect, always in flux—and the butcher was in control of his success given good treatment of his customers. The Socialist approach presumes the butcher will never figure it out and proposes that government set the price of pork for him, taking away his responsibility for success.

Christians and Socialists have a pessimistic attitude about the nature of man whereas the utopian designers' pure thinking and uber capabilities could design a perfect society that would enable man to reach their aspirations of perfection. This version of future history promoted the state as the mechanism that institutionalized rules that allowed humans to attain perfection. This presumes that some person or persons exist that are perfect or can design something perfect to overcome our shortcomings, individuals not being competent to overcome their deficiencies. This conceit leads to a very pessimistic few of the world. Men cannot improve themselves without the guidance of the special people populated in this special class of citizens, the dictators. So, though it is optimistic to believe that some of us are perfect, it is pessimistic to believe that the rest of us are incompetent without 'natural leaders' dictating the way to their perfect future.

For the Left, the commoners need to 'get with the program.' Marx's version of perfection, his Garden of Re-education, the Dictatorship of the Proletariat, is required to prepare citizens for the perfect Communist society. The intellectual conceit? That a special (maybe perfect) philosopher like Marx could create the perfect society and a perfect re-education camp to assure the perfection of those who would be citizens in his *Brave New World*. Marx's pessimistic attitude about both the proletariat and the bourgeoisie, that they had little or no ability to improve their lot, that the State must train them for the perfect society, left them at the mercy of a state with unlimited powers to subjugate the masses instead of improving them. Too much power in too few people does not make for a perfect society. Whether kings or dictators, the result is too much power in too few leaders.

The optimism of Adam Smith lay with millions of people who routinely improve their lives and those with whom they interact and enhance their lives. The Smithian approach requires no dictatorship to set a single course for humanity, just some basic rules of governance that we all agree upon.

Is the perfectibility of man possible? Maybe. Perfection, however, whether in an individual or institution or government, is an evolutionary journey, an exceptionally long journey, not 20,000 pages of complex regulations set in a point in time. This evolutionary and continuous human project is also much more of a bottom-up endeavor than a top-down endeavor. Not much is needed from the top, only a basic superstructure that maximizes our freedoms while minimizing bad players.

All too often, the endeavor from top-down leadership misses the opportunity to take advantage of the overwhelming numbers of individuals trying to improve their lives. The top-down push isn't from a lack of good intentions, but a pessimism about the commoners' ability to raise their game with little assistance. When individual optimists improving their station meet the pessimists hoping to control us meet, mediocrity, or worse—failure—often ensues.

How does perfectibility intersect with modern politics? It arrives at the intersection of the Socialist top-down pessimistic approach versus the bottom-up, optimistic, democratic Capitalist approach.

The Socialist approach believes that most of us cannot operate on our own without the helping hand, arm, and backbone of government. President Obama stated our deficit during the 2012 campaign, "If you've got a business, you didn't build that . . ." and "Somebody helped to create this unbelievable American system that we have that allowed you to thrive. Somebody invested in roads and bridges." Were Obama suggesting that government invest in just the foundation, the roads, this makes sense. The Left's objectives, though, are far more expansive for government and restrictive for our individual rights. The Left wing hopes to pass legislation that either states a right to something, or simply writes a check to gloss over the social problem believing that lack of money is our main challenge, not human capital. And what is written down, legislated by our leaders, are rights or privileges that are not owned by us. They are owned by the government, a dubious unfreedom by any measure.

The citizen is provided for whether help is needed or not. The government owns the responsibility for our success. Top-down and pessimistic, our natural leaders believe that government *knows* your needs and that government is required for your access to any level of success. Government is good, always! This is a bold conceit. Government can produce good results, but seldom does so when it assumes good intentions always produce good results. This pessimistic approach is great for growing government but not for encouraging individual responsibility for executing one's path to personal greatness.

Democratic Capitalists take a different approach. Most (not all) understand that the government does not need to legislate the rights you already enjoy because those rights exist without legislation. For example, no law states your right to purchase a car, or clothes, or food. The minimum input from government—generally environment regs and food nutrition labels—mean citizens have the right to invest in products as they please. The absence of law translates into the freedom from law, producing an absolute individual right.

The road to improvement via Democratic Capitalism is through opportunity which comes via the evolutionary idea cycle: idea, investment, income and profits, more ideas, more investment . . . and on and on. Bottom-up and optimistic translates into the fewest rules required to assure the smooth running of the idea-opportunity cycle for hundreds of millions.

Is there a balance between the pessimism of government-mandated perfectibility the Socialists hope to attain through top-down legislation and the optimism centered on the evolution of improvement via individual opportunity via Democratic Capitalism? There is, but a new perspective about how to use the wise organizational structure of a limited federal government is needed. Boiled down to its essence a twenty-first century approach, a Federalism 2.0, should revolve around evidence-based governance. If the data says a solution improves our lot and meets its objective, perfect. If it is not, start over.

Our leaders in Washington are stuck in the early twentieth century governance. The world changed and is changing more quickly. A government of the status quo that accepts mediocre results is becoming expensive, complex and harmful. Government that can evolve, change, update itself when its solutions do not meet objectives is optimal in a century when change is accelerating. The absent processes: testing to validate a hypothesis! When a solution fails or does not meet objectives, leaders need a hint of humility to admit failure and the flexibility to discover new ideas, even disruptive ideas with potential for better results. Execution comes via continual input and the testing of both current implementation as well as new ideas, persistent discovery for improved results, and the institutionalized pursuit of new evolving paradigms that will further improve our lives and our governance. These processes are impossible if government and our political parties believe current policies and programs are fine even if stuck in the pessimism, adamancy and poor results of their original thinking.

A little of both optimism and pessimism are needed to have great government. The question is how to arrive at a quality balance that restrains our pessimism and highlights our optimism. More on this later in the chapter titled: Challenges to Great Government, and a Fix!

Conclusion

Our three branches of government are like the executive suite in a business. Executives are needed, but they are a non-productive expense—overhead. A corporate income statement breaks out SGA (sales and general administration) as a separate barometer of financial success. These overhead expenses are required, but when they are too large, they produce a question mark for stock analysts. Consider the federal government is our nation's SG&A expenses. Government is a tax on our production. The bigger and more complex, the heavier the tax on our productivity. If government is optimistic about its citizens and their business endeavors, a smaller, more streamlined, less expensive SG&A results. An additional benefit arrives with less onerous regulatory environment. Pessimistic leadership moves the needle in the opposite direction, increases SG&A expenses as well as boosting the regulatory environment and its concomitant expenses.

Beware of the pessimist candidate who avers more central programming. Also be aware of the Pollyanna optimist that is a bit too cozy with big business, big labor and big money. Find the optimist that believes in the common man, the butcher, the baker, and the candlestick maker along with trust allied with trust but verify. A political leader's trust in those governed is a currency of great leadership. It's a two-way pact, and the next topic.

THE TWO-WAY TRUST CHALLENGE

FORMER SECRETARY OF STATE, GEORGE Shultz often said that, "Trust is the coin of the realm." Without trust, economies, societies, cultures and politics crumble.

No personal relationship, nor business relationship, nor any economic transaction occurs without trust. The more trust, the more likely that the cost of the transaction will be adjusted downward. Sixty years ago, 80 percent of Americans trusted government. Today, over 80 percent of Americans distrust government. The distrust of government is largely because the well-intentioned social programs that political parties marketed over the last ninety years have not produced results that worked as stated. After decades of political failure, it's hard to imagine that we have any trust at all in government.

Conversely, three quarters of consumers trust the brands they purchase. We trust the brands we buy, largely because the products we invest in meet our quality and price expectations. Global brand trust stands at 75 percent. A long history of buyer beware, or caveat emptor, or trust but verify, has worked well to keep the wolves our of our collective hen houses.

Why is there an enormous difference between trust in government and trust in business? With business, you get what you pay for. There is a direct feedback loop. When customers buy products that are as good or better than touted in commercials, they continue to buy the product. When they don't, they buy from a competitor. With government, promises are made, then ignored, then when failure arises, spin accelerates. No trust, no verify, not leadership.

With government, what you get is lots of talk and glittering generalities, poor service and high prices. Government, like any monopoly, does not listen well. Worse, when a delivered solution does not meet expectations, little is done to remedy the problem and politicians ask for more money, believing spending more will resolve any problem, which is a problematic request because for the consumer, quality and value are as important as costs. Americans will pay a premium for a great product, the iPhone. Many technology products we purchase have been less expensive over time or incorporate more features at about the same price. A 1980s style IBM computer sold for $5,000 and had a VGA monitor, 10MB hard drive and 64K memory. Today a pedestrian Lenovo with a $500 price tag has a 4K screen, 120GB solid state disk drive and 4GB of RAM. The cost of poor commercial products translates to 'out of business.' The cost of poor government translates to 'send me a bigger check.' For high performing organizations of any type, it's not how much you spend but how well the dollars are spent to resolve a problem. For example, Apple spent about $150 million to develop the iPhone. In 2007, first year sales topped 1.3 million iPhones. This year over 200 million were sold. Not a bad investment. Conversely, America spends $700 billion for schools, and though per capita spending has doubled in real dollars for the last forty years, the proficiency of students has declined slightly. The results are the same for poverty and retirement, lots of money spent but with poor outcomes. Apple created much trust in its brand by building a product that consumers continue to love. Is there a reason government can't and shouldn't do the same?

Both Socialist and corporate Capitalist approaches often produce policies and programs that decrease trust because solutions do not work as proposed. The pessimism that colors Socialism—that only government can help the citizen succeed—is built on a two-way negative feedback loop between the governed and our governors. When the politicians have a downbeat attitude regarding the capabilities of citizens, their pessimism fuels distrust and programs are built to overcome deficiencies of the citizenry. The 'I'm looking down my nose at you'—distrust—is captured by the citizen and returned in kind. A constant feedback loop surges between the leader and the voter which increases both pessimism and distrust.

Capitalist distrust shows up in contracts required for execution of business. Take the time to read the End User License Agreement for the software you buy online the next time you purchase software and the distrust of the buyer becomes apparent. It takes only a few seconds for your eyes to glaze over and realize the manufacturer does not trust you or the people that built the software. The legal squad guarding Capitalism's corporate fortress are no better than the same squad creating regulations in Washington. As noted earlier, Hernando de Soto explained the decreased productivity caused by the legal community; the two-way trust challenge is the same for Capitalists and Socialists alike.

Conclusion

Trust is hard to come by and it only takes one lie, one disingenuous spin, or one deflection to sweep our trust away. This is our position today because we tend to turn down the volume once a politician begins to speak, once the anger starts, and once the spin begins. Worse, our trust is further debilitated when the media and press report only one side of the story in support of the political party with which they have aligned. There is no single source of the truth.

The trust challenge has been abused by Socialist and Capitalist styles of governance and the lawyers who fill in the details in government regulation or business contracts. For either group, the question of trust is related to the associated risk. There is no easy solution, but the two differing government styles provide insight to what works and what does not, what we trust and what we do not, and what we enjoy and what we don't.

The IRS is a convoluted amalgamation of rules and credits (more 70,000 pages) so complex we worry that we are at odds when we file our taxes and that the next call will be from the IRS audit team. We don't trust the IRS and worry that our 1040 has an unforced error that produces, "Hi, I'm Joe from the IRS."

Not that our leaders are completely devoid of good leadership. The 1998 Internet Freedom Act, part of an omnibus spending bill, encompasses only two pages and places a moratorium on taxing the Internet. Simple. Smart. Few rules have created a trusted Internet environment with a few warts, whereas the IRS is both complex and uniformly reviled.

The two-way trust challenge with Internet brands has worked, if only be-cause the trust of both the consumer and the businesses they engage employ the light touch of government. The IRS's heavy hand and Congress's growing tax regulation has produced distrust of the agency with rules that seem to favor the rich, which by the way, they do. Our political monopolies, Left and Conservative, have also produced growing distrust among our legislators, spawning angry echo chambers that do not debate ideas. Distrust shuts off conversation.

The potential for trusting and trustworthy governance has been replaced by partisan power-mongering. With political monopoly power, not trust, as the guiding principle in Washington, the strategy of the Left often makes Conservatives complicit in poor governance, and vice versa. Distrust has produced increasingly divergent principles of government which creates more distrust, as there is little in the middle upon which to agree.

The result? Micromanagers proliferate in political leadership. Which leads us to the next section.

Who wins the contest of Socialist versus Capitalist government regarding trust? Neither, as power politics erases any hope of good governance.

COMPLEXITY VERSUS SIMPLICITY

SIMPLICITY IS SELDOM A PRIORITY when solving political problems. Legislative decisions generally devolve into committee decisions which all too often introduce amendments that may have nothing to do with the solution and are more about acquiring votes to pass legislation. Simplicity, though, is the essential element for designing and engineering new products or seeking the validation of a theory in science. Leonardo Da Vinci wrote that, "Simplicity is the ultimate sophistication." From our daily experience, *Keep It Simple, Stupid* is a constant reminder of simplicity's importance. The challenge for simplicity, then, is not that it should be a high priority but that complexity is so much easier to accommodate.

William of Occam (died 1347) provides insight about the importance of simplicity. This little-known friar is an important part of scientific thinking because of his clear-cut proposal: "Entities should not be multiplied unnecessarily." This is Occam's Razor, or law of briefness. His idea has been restated in several ways but is best understood as 'the simplest explanation is usually the correct one.' This principal cuts away, or slices and leaves aside, a host of potentially competing conclusions or arguments, leaving the simplest and most likely conclusion in place. The Razor is an indispensable element of any type of problem-solving in that "simpler solutions are more likely to be correct than complex ones." (Wikipedia.)

Business leaders like Steve Jobs of Apple, and Serge Brin and Larry Paige of Google were ardent devotees of simplicity, constantly reinforcing its importance on their teams when developers hoped to add more features to complicate products.

And it's not just products. In 2015, former Fortune 500 CEO, Bill

McDermott, suggested that the complexity of business processes in large companies ate up 10 percent of their costs. Imagine the complexity of our government, which is 250 times the size of the average Fortune business.

Complexity in government, whether local, state, or federal, produces challenges for every citizen. Hernando de Soto identifies the legal profession, especially lawyers in government, as the chief cohort of complexity enablers. In the *Mystery of Capital*, de Soto, describes how willful legislative complexity prohibits land ownership, even by those who have lived on the land for generations.

> The difficulty is that few lawyers understand the economic consequences of their work, and their knee-jerk reaction to extra-legal behavior to large-scale change is generally hostile. All the reformers I have met working to make property more accessible to the poor operate with the presumption that the legal profession is their natural enemy. Economists involved in reform have become so frustrated with legal conservatism that they have invested time and money to discredit the legal profession. Using economic data from fifty-two countries from 1960 to 1980, Samar K Datta and Jeffrey B. Nugent have shown that over every percentage point increase in the number of lawyers in the labor force (from, say 0.5 percent to 1 percent percent), economic growth is reduced by 4.76 to 3.68 percent, this showing that economic growth is inversely related to the prudence of lawyers. (Soto, *The Mystery of Captal,* 2000, p. 10)

Not only is it natural for complexity to increase as organizations grow, but government incorporates a double challenge as 40 percent of our legislators are lawyers who thrive on detail. When there is a problem, there is a propensity to over engineer it, as seen in the earlier examples, Obamacare, Medicare, our tax code, and our hundreds of thousands of pages which compose our regulatory state.

Why do our legislators take a simple problem and design a complex solution? Good question.

It may be helpful to reflect on the 2010 Dodd-Frank financial regulation that proposed a solution to the housing bubble that exploded in 2008. This 20,000-page regulatory expanse certainly gave banks the opportunity to hire an additional gaggle of lawyers to examine every commercial and investment transaction that transited their bank. The problem that caused the bubble in the first place, the root core problem, could have been executed on a single page of paper. What started the chain reaction that blew up the economy?

Why do these complex, over-reactions occur? Is it the propensity of lawyers who are legislators, as de Soto states, to be more verbose and controlling? Is it the natural pessimism and distrust of the Socialist approach to look past the simple solution to more central power via complexity? Whatever the issue, a Chief Simplicity and Innovation Officer for Congress might be a nice touch for legislators gone wild on micro-management activities to find the most complex solution possible.

Lawyers and legislators aren't so much the bad guys here, just myopic enablers of Progressive or autocratic legislators, building dysfunctional monopolies and legal edifices whose command-and-control organizations are run by more lawyers. Legislation, instead of being based on the economy and dynamism of the language found in the Bill of Rights or Constitution, is more like a giant legal mote built to protect a castle (government monopoly) with legal strictures that require and mandate barriers to success for citizens, providing little or no flexibility for freedom for the individual or innovation by the State.

The IRS and its 70,000+ pages of complexity provide a great example of complexity and a possible very simple solution.

Imagine a tax code that could be written on a single piece of paper.

Most proposals for tax simplification generally devolve into a discussion of what special deductions should remain. Rand Paul's 2015 proposal, which is the simplest offered, retains only the home interest deduction and charitable contributions. In 2017, the Trump administration said it simplified the tax code, but they only raised the standard deduction to a high enough level that 80 percent of tax filers had no need to itemize deductions. The number of pages of tax code did not decrease. But most candidates offer few changes to the complexity of the tax code, especially on the business side of the equation. Businesses have had an affinity for the 179 deduction for depreciation. Hedge fund managers like the preferential treatment of passive-type income. Elon Lusk loves the tax credits he gets from the feds and on car purchases and the $100s of millions selling regulatory credits that competing auto makers need for fuel-economy compliance. The list is long. Again, there are 80,000 pages of tax goodies for politicians' friends.

Do we really need all the special treatment? Shouldn't there be a Tom Lewellen deduction that makes me rich? Or a special deduction for you? Of course, there is not anything for you or me because we can't afford to pay the lobbyist to get our preferences appended to a bill. It is no wonder that most of us feel the country is going in the wrong direction because the deck is stacked against us. We have no sponsorship in our government.

The need for special tax benefits is also a benefit to the congressmen who want to get reelected and want a donation from some business or organization. Do we really need any of these deductions? Or is a totally flat playing field with respect to taxation a better formula. Although many politicos, wonks and beneficiaries of tax credits will cry wolf about a code with no tax breaks, a tax code that preferred no one would be much better, if only for the simplicity. According to Representative Dave Camp (R-Mich) the cost for filing taxes is high.

It takes the average American taxpayer 13 hours to comply with the tax code, gathering receipts, reading the rules and filling out the forms the IRS requires. ... The tax code forces Americans to spend over $168 billion to comply and 6 billion hours. (Kessler, 2015)

Though this is only about 1 percent of our total GDP, wouldn't an additional one percent of productivity be a nice gift to our slow economy. So how might a one-page tax code look?

Combining the three highest tax rates into one, gives us a handy way to view income and taxation in quintiles. These rates accommodate our 80,000 pages of tax regulations, credits, and deductions. These are 2014 tax rates by income as the newest research tabulation for 2019 were not available.

2014 Tax Rates: 10%, 15%, 25%, 28%, (33%, 35%, 39.6%)

The tax rates Americans paid, however, after taking advantage of all the deductions were:

2014 Effective Tax rate by quintile:

1.9%, 7.0%, 11.2%, 15.2%, 23.4% (Tax Policy Center, 2014)

Instead of wasting our time with trying to figure out all the giveaways, we should just pay the effective rates which produce exactly the same amount of tax revenue without the thirteen hours of pain required to fill out complicated tax forms.

For those who wonder which quintile they will likely fall under (and these quintiles do not exactly match up but are close enough to get a good idea of where you lay in the American economic landscape.

Average 2012 Household Income by Quintile:

$11,490, $29,696, $51,179, $82,098, $181,905 (Tax Policy Center, 2015)

For businesses, the option for a single rate would make for increased simplicity with a single tax rate and no special deductions. The corporate tax rate (2014) was 35 percent. The average tax rate across the twenty-four industries the IRS tracks was 12 percent, the rate varying from a low of around 3 percent for the construction industry to over 20 percent for retail and banking. Wouldn't it be nice, though, if an army of tax lawyers weren't required to navigate the tax code to find the best deductions, a neutral, flat tax being easy enough to compute so that the accounting department could do the taxes.

Simplicity has big payoffs. The flat tax approach for businesses would level the playing field for all businesses, neutralizing credits for special business interests. In a perfect, future world, where the government was about half its current size, a government that didn't have $100 trillion in unfunded mandates, a government that responsibly executed only its duties outlined in the Constitution, a single tax bracket would be possible, at around 8 percent or 9 percent. But this will only be possible when government decides to be simpler.

Simplicity, Complexity and Science

Science is so incredibly useful because from a treasure of data, hypotheses are proven. Even better hypotheses are uncomplicated. The simplicity of our universe is not easy to discover, but those who are patient and diligent will find simple patterns that divulge the complexity of our world. So too should be the efforts of wonks, intelligentsia and politicians, but, for reasons unknown, even the brilliant favor complexity.

An example may help. The following is culled from Siddhartha Mukherjee's *The Gene, An Intimate History*. In the chapter "The Book of Man" Mukherjee provides a beautiful description of DNA's simple structure to an amazing complex universe of human biology. The narrative provides a path from an extraordinarily simple code to an amazing evolving innovation engine. What follows, to keep it simple—is from three of the twenty-three bullets.

- It has 3,088,286,401 letters of DNA (give or take a few).
- Published as a book with standard-size font, it would contain just four letters—AGCTTGCAGGG . . . and so on, stretching, inscrutably, page upon page, for over 1.5 million pages—sixty-six times the size of the *Encyclopedia Britannica*.
- It encodes about 20,687 genes in total—only 1,796 more than worms, 12,000 fewer than corn, and 25,000 few genes than rice or wheat. The difference between "human" and "breakfast cereal" is not a matter of gene numbers, but the sophistication of gene networks. It is not what we have: It is how we use it.
- It is fiercely inventive. It squeezes complexity out of simplicity. It orchestrates the activation or repression of certain genes in only certain cells at certain times, creating unique contexts and partners for each gene in time and space, and thus produces near-infinite functional variation out of its limited repertoire.

Mukherjee's elegant story of DNA is not only a beautiful description of mankind's biology; it is a lesson for great leadership and even greater governance. Problem-solving is best when its understanding of the root core issue is well defined; there is a hypothesis; when the problem is well-understood; when there is adequate data; and when solutions are simple. Though DNA was first discovered by Swiss chemist Friedrich Miescher in the late 1860s, we are still understanding the incredible way it works. More from Mukherjee: *"Although we fully understand the genetic code – i.e., how the information in a single gene is used to build a protein – we comprehend virtually nothing of the genomic code – I i.e., how multiple genes spread across the human genome coordinate gene expression in space and time to build, maintain, and repair a human organism."*

The statements seem like fantasy because they are so amazing. From simplicity grandly complex solutions are possible. Our universe is similarly built on four variables: gravity, electromagnetism, the strong nuclear force and the weak nuclear force, all having precise mathematical relationships with one another. From these four building blocks, the universe banged into existence generating three elements hydrogen, helium, and lithium. From these elements, stars formed, then galaxies, then life itself. Aging stars fused hydrogen to helium and then all the elements up to the creation of iron. Energies in the stars' cores become unbalanced with the creation of iron, crushing stars into supernovas which created the remainder of heavy elements. Amazing. From simple structures to amazing complexity throughout the universe.

Should our laws, especially regulatory, industrial policy and social monopolies have similar simple foundations which are 'fiercely inventive' and which 'squeeze complexity out of simplicity.' They should. This approach, though, requires legislators and executive leaders (even lobbyists and the intelligentsia) who realize effective government that produces great results must start with the simplest approach possible, which creates a modest superstructure that plans for the competition and squeezes innovation from all corners of society.

Conclusion

Do both the Socialist and Capitalist approach to democratic governance have severe problems with complexity? Absolutely. Though the Socialist approach and its big government propensity builds complexity into problem-solving, the Capitalist habits that too often trend to corporatism (aka lobbyists) provide their own path to complexity (special regulations, tax for their friends) which is not much better than the Socialist approach.

Neither approach wins a check mark and advocates of both political parties need to take a lesson for what citizens almost uniformly understand, *Keep It Simple, Stupid.* There is more about how to overcome the complexity challenge in the section Challenges to Great Government, and a Fix.

SOCIAL JUSTICE VERSUS INDIVIDUAL JUSTICE

IF YOU BELIEVE IN OUR republican form of Democracy, a style of government in which citizens elect their leaders, then individual justice should be at the top of your political hierarchy of needs right after individual freedom. Social justice is a derivative of egalitarianism, an alternative path to Socialism. Conversely, individual justice is the centerpiece for Democracy and free enterprise. For instance, did George Floyd—murdered by Minneapolis police in 2020—need social justice and economic justice, or individual justice and increased human capital? The former would not have done Floyd much good. The latter meant he would have never been on the street in the first place, and the officer, because of his litany of problems, would have never been on the police force.

Social justice establishes the need for the distribution of wealth, opportunities, and privileges within a society—by the government. This is Socialism in its purest form and a derivative of the *Communist Manifesto*. The government knows how to run your life best and is responsible for executing policy to get citizens inside the lines of what the government thinks a right-minded citizen should be. Social justice mandates that individuality give way to the struggle for social justice. If you want a collective, instead of a collection of individuals, social justice is the political journey of choice. Welcome to Winston's Smith's world (*1984*).

When law attempts to overcome challenges of low income, low opportunity, and poor education by homogenizing them into a social framework, the road to one's pursuit of happiness is annihilated. Social justice, when incorporated into the Socialist approach assumes that people are poor and/or outside the envelope of justice because of lack of income and lack of standing in society. Sending a check or free services should fix the problem. Poverty and cultural displacement, though, are created and sustained by lack of human capital and the pivotal need is an education and a sound and safe family life. In other words, social justice warriors wish to define for the citizens some financial minimums for success, whereas individual justice is based on our unalienable right to Life, Liberty and the Pursuit of Happiness, and the freedom to execute these rights. The chasm between these propositions of governance is so vast, there is no middle ground. The warriors want redistribution of income to define happiness. The liberty team understands that our unalienable rights require a very level playing field that starts with a great education, by which any person can climb the ladder of success on their own terms and regardless of 'race, creed or color', and with focus on the 'content of their character.' Because social justice warriors who inhabit Congress, our state governments, and school boards aren't focused on absolutely guaranteeing a high-quality education, their go-to solution is sending money and free services to those 2/3 of students who do not get an adequate education. "Oops, we goofed. Sorry, here's your check."

Does injustice for certain groups exist? Injustice may be too convenient a word. A failure of leadership and governance may be more appropriate. Not only did the founding fathers fail three important groups—in particular Native Americans, women, and African Americans—but much of the legislative effort to remedy these challenges has all too often caused harm or simply missed the targets.

Regarding African-Americans, on the upside, the Civil War paved a new path for integrating blacks into our society. What the Civil War did socially—place African Americans as full citizens—was adopted legally in the Fourteenth Amendment assuring citizenship for blacks. As cultures are hard to change, and the depth of racism in the South prevailed despite the Fourteenth Amendment legal mandated for equality, the Civil Rights Act of 1964 overturned the social and legal underpinnings of Jim Crow laws in the south. The one remaining element of cultural inclusion, access to civil rights, did not fully materialize. Worse, a failure of thought regarding raising all social and cultural boats by social justice warriors from the 1930s on—that free checks and services would reduce poverty and a path to inclusion in the

American way of life—proved untrue.

In 1965, Democrat Daniel Patrick Moynihan, hired by President Lyndon Johnson to develop policy for the War 0n Poverty, challenged the status quo of the social justice warriors of his time in the Moynihan Report. He wrote: "The steady expansion of welfare programs can be taken as a measure of the steady disintegration of the Negro family structure over the past generation in the United States." Our social welfare approach to the black challenge harmed instead of helped the very people social policy hoped to remedy because the approach mistook redistribution of dollars instead of guarantee of increased human capital. Moynihan's voice was ignored by his party and the president, and all presidents since, regardless of party. The opportunity to transform a failing education and welfare system sixty years ago vaporized and to this day as the destruction of black families, and all poor families, continues. Social justice warriors will not give up on redistribution as the only method to achieve justice despite continued evidence and harm to African Americans and people of color.

More important perhaps, are events outside Congress that helped propel black culture. Jesse Owens captured the 1936 Olympics, beating the 'white master race' competitors from Hitler's Nazi Germany. What a wonderful and pivotal milepost. When Branch Rickey, signed Jackie Robinson for the Brooklyn Dodgers in 1947, the world changed and changed for the better. The number of individual efforts by both blacks and whites over the last eighty years are too numerous to list, but consider the grand effect of bottom up, from the smallest units of our social fabric, us, have occurred and have improved the more and more complete integration of African Americans into our culture. Each is an incremental test of our virtue and each improves our lives. That a black, white and Hispanic can hang out at a bar together is so vastly better than having a law that mandates this as the correct social construct under penalty of law.

For women, though some legal efforts made important changes; women largely took their needs on their own backs and changed their world. Though most social justice warriors state a fact that women earn 70 percent of what men earn, the other fact not mentioned is that when women work the same jobs as men with the same amount of experience, they earn 98 percent of men's pay. Ruth Bader's emergence in the 1971 Supreme Court Case to over-turn the unequal status of women's pay for like employment was pivotal. The application of the Fourteenth Amendment's 'equal protection' was also essential as is the nineteenth amendment, the women's right to vote. Is there still room to grow? You bet. But it seems women would have been better off fighting their own battles than having government muck up legislative micro-management.

The Native America community may have consumed the most harm. During the Reagan Administration, Secretary of Interior James Watt aptly described the challenge for native Americans. "If you want an example of the failure of Socialism, don't go to Russia, come to America and go to the Indian reservations." The limitations of property—all lands are owned by the tribe and not individuals—have produced a society that is desperately poor. This lack of land ownership is precisely the problem William Bradford solved in the Plymouth Colony in 1606 when he adopted individual responsibility for land versus the communal approach. Native Americans have a millennia-old tradition of communal land. Overcoming this tradition is no easy task. The federal government thought that bringing a profitable industry to the native reservations would help create wealth, and Indian Gaming was legalized in 1988 by the federal Indian Gaming Regulatory Act. Although it has produced $25 billion in annual revenues across 450 gaming sites, gaming has added little to the income of individuals or government services on the reservation or solved the inability of its citizens to own property. As reported during the COVID pandemic, many homes do not have water and Internet services are in short supply. How to overcome the Socialist challenge of no property ownership will be an enduring problem for both the government and the tribes. The land-ownership challenges Hernando de Soto described earlier in third world nations are akin to that of Native Americans. Without land ownership, creating wealth is exceedingly difficult if not fully responsible for the poverty on the reservations. Asking Native Americans to give up the tradition of their lands being owned by everyone, though it may be a good idea, does go against thousands of years of history.

Income Inequality Versus Human Capital Equality

Social justice warriors have produced great marketing about Income Inequality so much so that it is now part of a national conversation. Though income inequality is an interesting variable of our economic health, it is both a trailing indicator and its data is a bit fickle in its generation and interpretation. Regardless, from quiescence to prominence in the news, both Leftist and Conservative commentators entwine it routinely in their reporting.

Selected Nations from CIA Listing of Global Gini Co-efficient

Country -> Variable ↓	United States	Ukraine	Finland	Iraq
GINI	41.4	26.1	27.4	29.5
Billionaires	630	7	6	0
Billionaire Wealth	$4 T	$8 B	$12 B	0
Top 1% Income	$2.2T *	UNK	$10 B **	UNK
GDP	$21.4 T	$142 B	$268B	$234 B
Per Capital Income	$66,080	$13,700	$51,670	$11,310

Figure 1: The Challenges of Wealth and Income by Gini

*1.5 million earners
** 30,000 earners

Income inequality, though, is not a new subject. Corrado Gini, sociologist, statistician, and Italian fascist during World War II is the father of the inequality debate. In 1912 he developed the Gini Coefficient as a measure of income inequality. Fascism, like Nazism, is a type of Socialism with a Capitalist veneer. Nazism is a shortened version of National Socialism, the toughest challenge for those curious about what the Gini Coefficient means. As seen in the figure above, it is a statistical quagmire with national inequality indexes all over any chart. Poor nations and rich lie close to one another. For instance, the United States, the richest nation in the world, is within one percentage point of The Democratic Republic of the Congo, one of the poorest nations. Belgium and Kazakhstan have almost identical income inequality, though Belgium's per capital GCP is five times that of Kazakhstan. Income inequality, though, is vastly different than wealth inequality creation, which is a key driver for improving incomes. Perhaps an American-like 41.4 Gini is optimal because the typical worker in the lowest quintile of earnings makes more than the average worked in the 26.1 Gini of Ukraine. From the chart above an optimal Gini is not readily apparent.

Exploring additional national statistics does not provide additional clarity on what income inequality has to do with personal, corporate of national success. Given that social justice warriors are seeking a lower GINI, what about the GINIs in the former Soviet Union and Red China which floated between 26-29 and where no millionaires or billionaires existed. If taking away the riches of the rich is the objective, the result of Socialist nations was to make the rich poorer and the poor, poorer, too.

For GINI advocates, a single approach to solving the inequality problem has been progressive taxes that consume increased chunks of income and wealth. This is class warfare at its Marxian best which assumes that anyone with 'too' much money is either using it for their own benefit, abusing their wealth, or simply should not have it. It is most certainly true that accruing any income illegally or fraudulently, no matter its size, is unacceptable and jailable. But should Warren Buffet have his wealth and income seized? Or Bill Gates? Whether the reader likes Sundar Pichai, Mark Zuckerberg or Jack Dorsey, CEOs of Google, Facebook and Twitter, respectively, they earned their income and wealth legally and have made billions of people happy and more productive, including millions of people who own their stocks. Even better, they continue to invest their great wealth to create more and more high-paying jobs, and/or like Bill Gates have pledged their personal fortunes to charity. Giving more of their money to our government that has been terrible at investing our dollars seems shortsighted for anyone except power mongering politicians in Washington.

Is taking dollars from the rich and empowering government to redistribute dollars and services to the poor a better solution than figuring out how to increase the incomes of persons at the bottom by increasing human capital? It did not work in Communist nations and redistribution efforts have not reduced poverty in America. So, maybe not.

Pinker's *Enlightenment Now* adds insight in the chapter devoted to the discussion of Income Inequality. He states that the Gini Coefficient is a measure of income only and does not include transfer payments from government nor free government services. When transfers are included, America's GINI drops into the 20s. Another GINI-like measure is via the consumer power and the incredible value of the American dollar. In this case, the incredible buying power of the U.S. dollar produced a consumption-like GINI in the mid-30s.

If the GINI is interesting but not necessarily useful in our measure of economic success, what measures should both social justice warriors and democrat Capitalists seek to better understand the challenges to the poor? Three variables are extremely important: 1) wealth inequality, 2) income mobility, and 3) the human capital quotient (HCQ). HCQ is a variable that no economist or politician tracks, because it's an invention by this writer and is still off the radar. What is HCQ? Human Capital is our personal tool kit. It is the summation of all the variables that engineer our individual success economically and socially. Education is *the* primary driver. A good education along with the adoption of good social skills—our social IQ—translate into increased and family formation industriousness will almost universally assure that a person has at least enough success in their life to need no services from government. As noted earlier, the BLS reported families with two working adults and an education had a poverty rate of 1.3 percent. A figure of 1.3 percent is a worthy objective for a new War on Poverty which can only be accomplished by an absolute mandate for government to assure 100 percent of our children acquire an education in which they are proficient in the key job drivers for education: math, science, reading writing and history.

When HCQ increases, a worker's income mobility improves, potential for rising income and wealth increases, and the GINI coefficient declines. As education proficiency rises from generation to generation, marriage rate rises, criminal activity declines, and economic fitness increases.

Conclusion

Social justice warriors in Washington have not produced one education success story for those most in need since the federal government got involved in the 1960s. Nor has the War on Poverty, welfare, nor our retirement systems been operated in a way that produce either social results or financial sustainability. Have their efforts been executed with the best of intentions? Yes. Should good intentions require good results, great results? Yes and Yes and Yes. Without good-to-great outcomes, great harm is done. Government becomes an even heavier tax on our productivity. Conversely, neither have Conservatives, nor individual justice warriors, produced great results, nor even good results. Both ideologies have failed to provide parents the unabridged ability to secure a quality education, financial sustainability for our social or health programs, or innovative thinking about how to better operate our government. Some efforts have been made for providing parents with new education options, like charter schools. A focus on work for welfare recipients has increased incomes. But neither political party's approach to governance has produced positive net social or cultural results. America has flopped back and forth between two poorly executed strategies.

Both political parties have hurt—not helped—the poor because both parties cling to the top-down, micromanaged approach dictated by a strong, central government associated with the big, complex, pessimistic, Socialist approach. America can do better.

There is no long-term strategy – economic, social or political – to accommodate either Capitalists or Socialists. Nor has there been policy from either political ideology that has produced continually improving results, only a continuing decline of financial and social metrics. There is a long historical track record for individual justice and personal responsibility as well as a long record of social engineering that has created evolutionary decline. The path to a common political strategy doesn't seem to be in our future. Perhaps Independents will take the stage and create a path that understands that greatness begins with the individual and focus on human capital will bring all groups together under the title of American.

VOTING, THE MORE THE BETTER

VOTING IN AN ELECTION IS truly an empowering event in our lives. Though there is no right to vote in the constitution, the election process belonging to the states, an especially important right is in the constitution. That right is the ability of any citizen to run for the House of Representatives, the Senate and for president. In 1787, when the constitution was ratified, the right for a commoner to run for office existed nowhere in the western world. Most elites across Europe thought empowering the commoner to vote for leaders was a little nutty. Commoners, were, you know, common. Allowing commoners into the circle of leadership was unthinkable. The elites looked down their noses and thought the America experiment would fail. Oh, how wrong they were.

Voting is much more than an exercise of political markets or legislative process. We vote for everything that touches our lives. Daily, we vote for products and services to determine what works best for us. We vote for which church to attend, what nonprofit to donate to, what news organization to read, view or listen to, whether to attend a protest, and what baseball team to root for. The luckiest get to choose what school their children attend or what doctor they prefer, but our choices in these categories are limited by government. We vote on everything and every ballot we cast, political or otherwise, is analyzed with great vigor. The vote getters want to understand why we choose them, and those that did not get your vote want to understand your choices even more. The leaders of Apple want to understand your vote to buy an iPhone as much as Trump or Biden hope to understand your vote. In the twenty-first century, the ability to dissect votes has reached incredible heights.

The freedom of our economic vote long before your political vote, emerged centuries ago with the coinage of money, bartering of goods, the budding provisions for property ownership, and both local and international trade that provided markets for more and more affordable products. What was a trickle of economic voting in the Middle Ages became a flood in the Renaissance, and a tsunami in the twenty-first century? Today, our economic votes are cast daily and in large volumes. The consumers' vote determines which products survive the marketplace as well as product pricing. Pricing? Consumer votes clarify whether prices increase or decrease as supply and demand vary. If consumers are not buying, pricing goes down. When demand is high, prices may increase. Your demand for products determines the price.

The more votes consumers have, the more likely products will increase in quality, pricing adjusting with demand. The fewer competitors in a market, the fewer votes we can cast, and the less likely price and quality will modulate in our favor. Politics is a market of products and the political parties have become a legislated duopoly. The number of laws to protect the Democrat and Republican monopolies is vast and each time a new entrant sees a bit of success, election laws increase the barrier to their entry. As 60 percent of voters believe neither party represents them, dissatisfaction with political products is on the rise if only because of the lack of choices. As the price of government increases, the quality of government wanes. Typical market forces should produce quite the opposite effects, but because of the political parties' monopoly on power, there are no choices to improve the effectiveness of federal leadership. Our votes go to leaders for more government and less effectives, no matter the party.

The price and quality of American-made cars in the 1970s were questionable. Like our political parties, our choices were limited to Chevrolet, Ford and Chrysler. These companies had a quasi-monopoly. Then, along came Japan. When Japan's lower priced and better built cars hit the market, the Big Three (Chrysler, Ford and Chevy) had to change, and they did, and consumers benefited from the additional choices of products for which they could vote.

When Walmart entered the consumer grocery marketplace, our choices dramatically changed. Traditional retailers like Kroger and Albertsons had to find ways to compete with Walmart's lower pricing and advanced supply chain management. They did, but many others went out of business. When

Southwest entered the airline market with low class, first-come, first-serve seating, the traditional competition poohed-poohed their approach. In the mid-1990s I was lucky enough to sit next to the CEO of America West during a flight back east. He lamented what looked like the end of first-class flyers, noting that when first-class was full, the flight was paid for and the coach flyers were profit. Competition from Southwest meant the other airlines had to change their strategy. The consumer won out. Telecommunications, air transportation, freight and shipping, and every industry has improved as options for our vote increased, and the consumer benefited.

And we vote. We call it shopping, but it is voting. The more choices we have, the more we love our opportunity to vote. A little competition might improve our political parties!

Plan for the competition, not against it.

Monopolies and the Vote

When our opportunity to vote is diminished, pricing and quality go to hell in a handbasket. There is a single source that deprives us of voting and diminishes the competition for the vote (whether economic or political): government regulation that plans against competition and government monopolies that provide a single solution. Both suppress our vote. Education, retirement, health care, and even anti-poverty programs which are one-size-fits-all are a result of one vote, one time. It has been nearly impossible to change or update any of these programs. Though predominately passed during administrations when Democrats had large majorities in the House and filibuster-proof majorities in the Senate, changes, or updates to improve services have been all but impossible.

Most voters are not old enough to have voted for these programs nor the persons that were elected to Congress to pass them. We are a Republic, not a Democracy, which is good. Short of a voter political revolt that tosses these parties to the curb, we are stuck with ineffective programs and strategies that do not measure up to the well-intended persons that engineered these solutions. These solutions are built into solid rock and impervious to change.

Sadly, no options include a new political party or parties that might fix these aging systems, because the political parties own the political monopoly and state politicians own the rules that create the barriers to entry to the political marketplace. Instead of planning for the competition, politicians plan for their perpetual ownership of power and the lamentable state of our social monopolies. The barriers to entry to the political marketplace are so high that no new political party has penetrated the Republican and Democrat political duopoly since the formation of the Republican Party in 1854.

Without new political options, your vote is compromised. With billions spent on elections to assure the continuance of the status quo, our votes are more about politically generated anger than about visions of smarter government.

Conclusion

Most American products and services are relatively free and open—Internet and cell services, apparel, housing, food, automobiles, power tools, and a long list of other commodities in which we have a wide variety of choices and limited number of regulatory guidelines. Competition keeps pricing affordable and it keeps the need for innovation high. In the areas where government has planned against competition, choices have waned and quality has diminished including schools, health care, and retirement as has been previously mentioned.

The biggest marketplace in which limited choices does the greatest harm is politics where the players that own the means of production also own the governmental processes to make law and regulation. Democrats and Republicans alike legislate for their continued dominance erecting significant barriers to new parties and new candidates that challenge the status quo of their own parties. Call it the Socialist approach to politics. Political monopolies are killing American opportunity. The two-party system is a great system, but only if you have two great parties. At this point, our political competition looks more like Studebaker and Edsel, than Apple or Amazon.

CENTRAL PLANNING OR
A STRATEGIC PLAN

A SUBTLE ECONOMIC DEBATE RAGED in the early part of the twentieth century between Maynard Keynes and Friedrich Hayek. Keynes's *General Theory of Employment* recommended higher levels of government borrowing with central planners creating jobs to achieve full employment. The jobs, according to Keynes's need not be productive. A fellow economist suggested an example – one man digging holes and another filling the holes. Hayek's *Road to Serfdom* promoted quite the opposite view. Too much central planning was problematic. Though Hayek wrote Keynes of his concerns about the central planning by government, he did not articulate what level of government intrusions were reasonable. What is 'Just Right'?

Hayek did articulate a good answer, though it does not appear his message was transmitted directly to Keynes. Hayek did not like government planning in any form but recommended, as quoted previously, planning *for competition not against it*. He also wrote: The more the state *plans,* the more difficult planning becomes for the citizen or a business.

Planning is both problematic and needed. The problems? First, plans are for the future, so there is an information problem because no information about the future exists. There are only guesses based on past information. Is it possible for government with limited resources to accumulate enough information to architect a plan with lasting impact? Of course not. Not only is there never enough information, but the stream of new information is vast and the nature of the data in that stream evolves over time. Change is a constant challenge. Nineteenth century, Prussian Field Marshall, Moltke the Elder, hit the nail on the head: "No plan of operations extends with certainty beyond the first encounter with the enemy's main strength." The first response of any warrior or competitor or government leader requires the plan to change. Planning is defeated by the evolution of ideas and our daily votes to update our preferences and provide direction for the evolution of our preference. Mike Tyson, world heavy weight champion, added a sportsman's view of planning. "Everyone has a plan until they get punched in the mouth."

Government has an additional planning problem. Governments are slow, stodgy, and lethargic, and they focus on the status quo, not the future nor innovation. The ability is nil for public institutions to change a plan in real time, much the way a business does in a competitive marketplace, or that we as individuals do when an unexpected bill shows up, or we lose a job. Non-existent. Hayek's guidance that government should plan for competition supports change, not only for private markets but for governance where change is avoided or ignored. Markets and market players must evolve or die. Investments, jobs, and profit follow a changing marketplace. Historically, government plans have been carved in rock and follow political decisions, not financial or social results.

Over the last forty years, much of the data available to both businesses and government is dark data, data stored in servers in the basement, and which is very difficult to access, and seldom consumable in real time. During the last decade, however, the increasing power of computing paired with vastly improved analytical tools, new and aged data can be organized and reviewed to produce amazing insights about the past which provides some predictive power of the future. Adding AI and Machine Learning, this new analytical world has produced enormous benefits to business and consumer alike. The government, though, is still grandly behind the information curve. As businesses are better able to plan with better access to data and better real time insights, they are not only able to plan better, but they also become more agile in changing a plan once the first marketing shot is fired. Whereas government plans are locked in legislative concrete and handicapped by dark data, businesses are making strategic changes in days or hours. Our government is governing from a different century.

Government does have hordes of data, but little is available in real time because of the low-quality of information technology infrastructure that is in place to analyze the data and provide insights. Were the information tools available, the focus of analysis should be on the net impact of current government programs and their financial and social results, *not central planning of the economy.*

Is a national plan needed and a good plan, a flexible one? The answer is, *yes, absolutely.*. The type of plan is important. A five-year central plan like the Soviets produced? A central industrial plan driven by government investment a la the Chinese plan for a command economy? The Chinese believe that a command economy is the competitive answer to open and free market competition. Their gamble is that they can outgrow the American economy by dominating specific markets: AI, pharma, manufacturing, rare metals, etc. Their approach may win, but they will win only if America proceeds without a strategy for future growth. How would this be different than a Chinese Five-Year Plan, or a series of five-year plans focused on top-down industrial imperatives? A set of strategic goals and some tactics will help get us there. An example may help.

In 1982, a fellow University of Arizona graduate and I decided to attend a basketball game to see what new head basketball coach, Ben Lindsay, would bring to the campus. Lindsay had a great record at NCAA Division 1 Grand Canyon University and won a national championship as well. My friend and I were pumped. The former coach, Freddie Snowden, had left the university and we were both hoping that Lindsay would take a step up the success ladder. The game, however, was a disaster. We got thumped. Our conversation after the game could be summarized as, "Nobody seemed to know what they were supposed to be doing." It looked like a pickup game, our players shooting at will, without passing, screening, or communicating, and then playing poor defense or no defense at all at the other end of the floor. There seemed to be no plan, no strategy for winning, no structure, no nothing. The Cats record did not improve as the season progressed, the Wildcats going 1-17 in the PAC-10. Ben was fired.

His strategy: Get good players and presume that their superior abilities would defeat the competition. If Lindsay had a broader plan, it was not apparent. He seemed to presume the tools for competition, the talent of his players, were sufficient to win the competition.

Lute Olsen replaced Lindsay the next year. For those who are not familiar with Lute, he had a plan, a strategy, and structure for evaluating the talent he recruited, how he ran practices, daily player data and rating that prioritized who started and who did not, and how he prepared strategy for each game. Players road the bench if they lofted ill-advised shots or did not play tough defense. With 60 percent of his scoring coming from Ben Lindsay's recruits who stayed with the team, Lute went 8-10 in a very tough PAC-10 and a particularly challenging non-conference schedule. The following year, the Cats were 21-10 and went to the NCAA tournament. Over 24 seasons at the UofA Lute's team won 22 PAC titles, 24 NCAA Tournament visits, 5 final Fours and one National Championship. Planning and strategy matter. It's the only way to win.

Did Lute created a five-year plan with details for any and all contingencies? Probably not, though it is clear he had wanted to build a program that could win a national championship which does not happen in a single year. Having a big goal is essential to creating a good tactical strategy. He did have strategy with key success tactics that worked. And he had a track record that showed his approach worked. Did he arrive at these tactics on the first day he became a coach? Not likely. On the other hand, Lute was one very highly organized person. He had a sound vision to build from, having learned from coaches he worked under, but it took time for the strategy and tactics to solidify. Lute was planning for the competition, in every way and for every game, and, importantly, *during* every game. Great coaches change the game plan as original plans fail, even during the game. Like Tyson, sometimes the plan fails with the first punch.

Do we, as a nation, need a plan, and a good one? Absolutely. With warnings from Hayek, Elder and Tyson as guidance, whatever plan is created, it needs flexibility. America needs a plan built from national objectives with strategy and tactics that can be tested and adapted and transformed when needed. Coach Lindsay had tactics that worked in Division II or III but not in Division I where the talent is high, and the competition is great. In a word, his approach was *laissez-faire*. The world economy used to be dominated by a couple of dozen Division 1 nations with America at the top. Competition was friendly and the rules were well understood. For Ben and America, a *laissez-faire* approach worked when the competition was NAIA Division VII.

China changed international competition. America is no longer competing with England or Germany or Japan economically. Though great economies, they are a fraction the size of America's. China has four times the population of the United states, so they four times the economic ability of other nations. Worse, the competition is no longer a friendly competition. More problematic China's rules of economic engagement do not accommodate the western nation's playbook. They have a common strategic goal: end US economic and military dominance and kick western civilization to the curb. The competition has risen from Division VII style play to Division I. China is changing the game to their favor as best they can, and America doesn't have a plan beyond sitting on our hands and hoping for the best. Hope is not a strategy, nor is hope a plan.

China has a strategic, tactical, and central thirty-year plan.

We do not. We don't even have a goal, an economic target that would minimize the Chinese economic onslaught.

Over the last 200 years, economic competition was both friendly and smallish. Great Britain was a partner and only a fraction the size of our economy. Ditto for Japan, Germany, and France. China is different. They have four times the population of the United States and they have a plan to kick us out of First Place in the Economic Sweepstakes. Theirs is not a friendly competition. China is increasingly aggressive economically, politically, culturally, socially, and militarily. They want to replace the template for western democracies' leadership with a Communist totalitarian paradigm along with a patina of Capitalism to fund their aggressive plan to replace western thinking and governance with totalitarianism and a command economy.

Copying the Chinese Socialist approach, even without the oppression of its people, is not a reasonable path for America. China clarified its harsh intentions through progressively aggressive action: sending Uyghurs to 'reeducation centers'; redefining security laws in Hong Kong to eradicate their autonomy; military exercises in the South China Sea; challenges to international boundaries; and non-stop theft of intellectual property from the West. China is, then, both a competitor, and a national security threat not unlike what the Soviet Union represented during the cold war. Will its increasing international belligerence and domestic heavy-handedness work to sustain high growth and to support their strategic, central plan? Time will tell but hoping their oppressive ways will mitigate their economic growth is not a good plan. Hope never works the way you want it to.

America's competitive stance should not attempt to be more like China's command economy nor its hostility toward its people. We do, though, need to understand how China could succeed when every other Communist venture in history has failed.

Under Deng Xiaoping's leadership in the 1980s, China made a huge constitutional change regarding the ownership of property that completely changed its Communist countenance. In doing so, it committed a Karl Marx no-no. Marx stated flatly in the *Communist Manifesto*: "The theory of the Communists may be summed up in the single sentence: Abolition of private property." Property is the foundational element of Capitalism, so it is little wonder that the exclusion of property is first on the list of requirements for the dictatorship of the proletariat. After Mao Zedong died, Deng challenged the property deficiency of Socialism, its inability to generate ideas via *'large numbers of path breakers who dare to think.'* To overcome this deficiency, China updated their constitution to allow for ownership of property, especially business ideas (intellectual property), stock, and capital, albeit suborned to the state. This tiny lean-in toward Capitalism provided the fuse that lighted China's spectacular economic rise over the last forty years. The new approach, Communism with a layer of Capitalism, is not unlike the national Socialism of World War II Germany or corporatism in Italy, where Capitalism was allowed, even encouraged, just under the thumb of the state. If China learned one thing from the demise of the Soviet Union, North Korea, and Cuba, it was that strict adherence to the first tenet of Communism, abolition of property, annihilated Socialism's ability to compete with free markets based on property rights and the importance of the individual's right to own property, especially ideas that created businesses and new markets.

This new Capitalist approach to Communism has been wildly successful for China, though the government is still run by a band of regressive Communists. Their economic success, though, makes China a huge risk to western civilization. Why? Over the next thirty years, China's stated, strategic plan will produce a faster growth rate (est. 6 percent) which will outpace the

United States (est. 2 percent.) The result: Their economy will be twice the size of America's giving them double the financial wherewithal to dominate the world economy, international political policy, and military influence. As former Director of National Intelligence John Ratcliffe noted in December 2020, China, beyond being an economic threat, is America's "No. 1 National Security Threat." Big GDP translated into big problems.

How does America counter China's Communism with a little Capitalism? The Ben Lindsay approach might work if the Chinese competition were friendlier, but China has been anything but friendly and the richer they have become the more belligerent they have become. We need a little Lute Olsen. Or John Wooden. Or Coach K. We need first rate players, but we also need to restate our goal, an international championship! Hayek's liberal economics, a *laissez-faire* approach to strategic national goals works when the competition is friendly but may fall short when the competition is telegraphing their desire to kick us to the curb. We need long-term goals for economic growth, and we need the winning strategy and tactics to meet our objectives. The foremost objective must be how we grow fast enough to keep China at bay. That number is a rolling ten-year average of 4.5 percent.

Though both political parties have identified the Chinese economic onslaught as a problem, not a single person in Washington has stated an economic growth objective. Many have touted spending objectives, but without associating how much growth, or degrowth, results from the spending. Government by non-objective is no government at all.

The challenge western Socialist planners face when attempting either a five-year plan or an industrial plan is how dollars should be invested and/or doled out by elected officials who have no risk in the success or failure of the investment. Second, few politicos have experience in business ventures nor the fiduciary responsibilities—evidence-based business decisions—that are central to the world of private investment. If a government investment fails, no person or person or parties in government is ever responsible. The taxpayer is left with the bill and a smaller paycheck. Most public investment does not produce even adequate results. Our public investors are risk free which makes them extremely poor financial stewards.

Conversely, big spending has one great political advantage. It buys votes.

Though poor results in education, retirement, climate, and anti-poverty have been mentioned repeatedly, if only because of the size of their underperformance, the federal spending spree has expanded during COVID with the 'stimulus' bills by both Trump in 2020 and Biden in 2021. They are great examples of spending that makes the rich richer. With three quarters of remarkably high growth from July 2020 to March 2010 (33.1 percent, 4.5 percent, 6.8 percent), instead of focusing on relief for those is the greatest need, hundreds of billions of dollars in checks to individuals generally unharmed by COVID flooded the economy. Most stimulus dollars were saved, used to pay down debt or flushed into the stock market, driving up stock prices—making the rich richer. Hundreds of billions of dollars went to other programs that had nothing to do with COVID. This shotgun approach to government is certainly not the scientific Socialism by any standard as its 'go big' tenet is if you don't know what to do specifically, do everything in the most expensive fashion possible to see what sticks and works. This is sloppy government, public investment gone awry from both Socialist and Capitalist approaches.

To further weaken the value of any public investment, when dollars begin transit from public to private sector, the target industry stagnates. The industry becomes locked in concrete. Then vested and public monied interests work diligently to assure no competition leaks into the market, killing innovation. In 1800, this approach may have worked as industries lasted for a hundred years with only tiny steps in innovation. By 1900, the average Fortune 500 company had a life span of one hundred years. In the twenty-first century, innovation is so rapid that the Fortune 500 lifespan has dropped to nineteen years. More competition will drive more innovation, so we need to plan for the competition in a manner that allows new disruptive ideas to thrive.

America and western nations need a plan. We don't need a five-year plan. We don't need an industrial plan that dictates which markets will get preferential treatment. We do need a plan that states our economic goals clearly and government transformations assures we reach our goal.

First, America needs neither a big government nor small government, but smart government. Our political parties run our government like a money machine with no restraints instead of a valued enterprise whose maxim is, "Spend the least amount possible to get the greatest effect."' The current mantra is, "Spend the most, with least effect but most votes."

The federal government is the worst-run organization in the world, and the biggest. Too many promises have been made and too little money is available to pay for the promises made by politicians over the last ninety years. Our retirement systems send $300 billion to top 5 percenters most of whom have enough wealth to sustain themselves without any help from government. On a Fox News radio show, one billionaire lamented that, *"I get a $3,000 check each month from Social Security, why I don't know, I don't need it."* Add in other tax credits and tax advantages to free money and services to the rich and the tally easily exceeds a trillion dollars. To add to rich person's government-made privilege, our public education system is set up to assure the rich get a great education, but the poor get shuffled to schools that have been failing for decades. Lastly, our anti-poverty programs are not designed to reduce poverty—and they have not. They need change. Transforming these three operational nightmares, excising the dollars to the rich and increasing the human capital for the poor, this year's budget would have been $3.2 trillion instead of $4.8 trillion. The goal of a best run, smart government will vastly reduce government spending providing a large pool of dollars for consumers and businesses because of diminished taxation.

Second, any plan (and our government operations, including legislative processes) must be more entrepreneurial and responsive to change. Bureaucracies and Congress must be more entrepreneurial, producing new processes and laws that are flexible and bend to allow for change instead of being locked in concrete and immune to change.

Conclusions

Socialist central and industrial planning are not a good idea for any nation. How China's plan to both create industrial favorites via crony darlings and, over the last five years, a heavy totalitarian hand on its people, remain to be seen. Will new social strictures diminish their Socialist economic planning and by how much? Time will tell. America's Capitalist approach on markets and *laissez-faire* imbued with Socialist monopolies and unbridled spending without any requirement for results diminishes the federal government's financial and social responsibilities as steward and fiduciary.

Whether Socialist or crony Capitalist, much of the 'planning' provided by political parties' advocates providing advantage to select groups of people, all too often their rich friends, big business, and donors. Worse, most planning is very short-term guided by two-year election cycles, then locked, loaded, and protected by big money from status quo patrons and, therefore, well-protected from change. This approach is exactly what China is doing, yet many complain about their intrusion into markets while other politicos recommend Socialist central planning is what we should emulate.

Both Democratic Capitalists and Democratic Socialists fail at planning. Neither approach scores in this competition. Neither party has a plan for competing and winning against China. Neither party has a plan to improve the finances of our government nor develop the human capital of those citizens most in need.

Plan for the competition, not against, would be advice well taken. Creating a long-term goal for growth and the tactic to achieve those results is essential. A proposed plan follows in *What's the Plan?*

THE END OF SOCIALISM.; THE END OF CAPITALISM

Is SOCIALISM AN EFFECTIVE FORM of government?

Examples of its strongest form, Communism, have been utter failures. Partial Socialist states, like Venezuela, show that as state players assume control over more and more private enterprise, profits go to political insiders, or friends that favor the autocrat, instead of being used to improve private enterprises from which they originated. This is the fatal result of dictator knows best. Even the Socialist approach in western nations, like our own, under the guise of big government and/or crony Capitalism—big government that 'knows best' the needs of individuals and business—tends to place investment in politically friendly enterprises that alter capital flows, which ultimately slow innovation and economic growth. Government's extensive investments in social programs have not produced desired financial or social outcomes. Socialism or even the democratic Socialism we vote for in western nations has not delivered quality education for all, quality public health care, nor reductions in poverty. Even our efforts to assuage climate have done little to affect global temperature, the mother's milk of climate Socialists. Put another way, as David Ricardo stated two hundred years ago, public assistance even with the best intentions makes the poor, poorer and the rich poorer too. A better approach might be, as John Kennedy recommended, "A rising tide lifts all the boats."

It is extremely hard to imagine why Socialism has not died a natural death except that very well-educated, highly intelligent people, with little common sense and lots of money and hubris, find the philosophy so extremely attractive if only because of the power it delivers for themselves, the American elite. Socialism has been in a continual death knell since its inception but continues to find new purchase in a continuing stream of politicians seeking power from our votes bought with big political donations and big government spending. This has translated into endless spending of big government dollars without big results—at no risk to our leaders' personal treasure—all to acquire your vote whereby increasing their political power. It is the kind of power grubbing of which they accuse Capitalists, except it is 'other people's money' they are spending.

Of the many variables of economy and Democracy discussed in this primer, just two demonstrate the greatest liabilities of Socialism: 1) the Socialist approach is a diminisher of ideas. Government spending on fixed social monopolies and borrowing to fund them reduces the capital available to private enterprise (idea generators) which slows economic growth and harms the worker at the bottom of the economic totem who has less access to employment and/or increased wages; and 2) the one-size-fits-all monopolist solutions diminish consumer choice, reduce quality, and increase costs. The Socialist approach we vote for is autocratic and aristocratic at its heart and it is a diminisher of financial and social objectives not a multiplier.

Government as a Socialist Enterprise

As the federal government legislates nationally, policy and program execution lead to the erection of a monopoly and ownership of means of production by government and thus is Socialist in its very genesis. The bigger and stronger government grows, the more Socialist the enterprise(s) becomes.

Government, too, is a monopoly as it owns the means of production of our laws, policy, and regulations. Constitutionally mandated responsibilities like the military and the judiciary are monopolies. As Congresses and presidents have adopted new responsibilities beyond constitutional requirements (such as Social Security, Medicare, etc.) these programs incorporate the means of production including employees, revenues, disbursements, and the legal framework for the policy. Over the last one hundred years, a rapid expansion of government's acquisition of new powers and new social programs have moved our limited federal government to a strong central government with a Socialist personality. As government powers increase, it becomes more autocratic.

When government adopts new responsibilities, especially once the means of production are owned by government, the missing planning component has been that there is no exit strategy when objectives are not met, nor transformations incented to improve outcomes. As government will never go out of business short of a revolution, it is vital that flexibility be part of the design, even to the point that an exit from the program is more reasonable than continuation.

Government is like any institution, business or nonprofit. Its strategy is to increase its span and size. Most of the federal government's social policies have employed a land-and-expand strategy to Socialist monopolies which increases program span and costs despite neutral or declining results. Social monopolies were they to work well should need fewer and fewer government resources. For example, if our anti-poverty programs worked, fewer people should suffer in poverty. This has not been the case for our War on Poverty.

Other Socialist approach challenges exist. As we have seen over the last couple of years, the cancel squad is also out to limit the marketplace of ideas in the economy, society, and culture, and even politics. The intolerance of the religious right during the 1980s is mimicked and enhanced by the secular theists on the Left, today. The cancel culture is not inhabited by secular priests with robes nor brown shirts, but illiberal pink shirts using twenty-first century megaphones, the Internet and cell technology, to enforce their narrow thinking.

The freedom to have and own ideas is increasingly important to a successful economy. Without a healthy economy, society, culture, and politics suffer. The notion that the voter can simply hand over the construction of our economy or society or culture to politicians may not seem unreasonable when candidates tell us they will change the world. This message sounds great. Execution of one-size-all programs and policy have not served us well, though, and has all but destroyed the cultures of people of color and the Forgotten Man.

The American Socialist approach creates a big government that has an elite-driven, top-down, micro-managed, *expert*-driven philosophy which has laid a sleepy haze over American exceptionalism. A political friend, Cordero Holmes, a young man of color that has had numerous challenges in life but who is a great believer in personal responsibility, put it this way: "American leadership is becoming like crazy King George." He was the King of England during the Revolutionary War whose heavy governance weighed crucially on America's decision to opt for independence and freedom.

When the founding fathers deliberated on the style of government in the Constitution Convention, a resolve to discuss a national government was voted down. Of national government and their leaders, kings and queens entwined with popes, Jefferson commented to George Washington, "There is scarcely an evil known in their countries which may not be traced to their king as its source, nor a good which is not derived from the small fibers of republicanism existing among them." He added that 'crowned heads' could not be elected vestryman in America. Vestryman roughly translates to dogcatcher today. The convention summarily voted down a national approach to government which gave way to a limited federal government that would have distributed all powers not vested in the Constitution to the states and the people. The king, like today's Socialist elites, thinks of citizens in flyover America as commoners that need herding from a strong, central government, not freedom from a limited federal government.

The challenge with Socialism is that as a national government—a strong central government and owner of social monopolies. The approach has been to replace the King George and the nobility with modern elites, experts, and secular theists. The only difference between one style, a national government with nobility, and the other, a national government driven by elites, are the titles. The challenge for both Socialist and Capitalist leaders in Washington is that they simply do not have enough ideas—nor common sense—to lead much of anything devolving to policies that extend their own needs, their own power. Worse, even though producing far too few ideas, their intellectual conceit or fondness for their lofty status locks their ideas in stone while the world changes around them.

Will Socialism ever die? It seems unlikely. If classrooms and professors who were never at any economic risk, or fantastically rich Capitalists that influence politicians to do their bidding, elitist, centrist thinking will have purchase if only because of the potential for accruing power.

Capitalism: An Evolution of Everything

Capitalism for all its warts, constantly evolves, creating and enhancing ideas and tossing bad ideas to the curb. When done well, and in conjunction with evidence-based governance, it is self-healing and inventive. Capitalism is an idea engine for which we all vote every day to help determine what ideas stay, what ideas will improve old ideas, and what ideas are past their shelf date. Capitalism has matured, evolved on its own, and when warts are identified, good policy reduces the wart problem. That government regulations do not always meet the smart and simple sniff test, and many regulations are overdone, time generally provides the evolution of ideas to help correct excesses. Capitalism today has vastly fewer warts than its nineteenth century version with monopolists and hoarders like Scrooge.

Will Capitalism die? Schumpeter suggested the end of Capitalism may occur. He wrote, "Can capitalism survive? No. I do not think it can." His explanation left the door open for its continued existence, if only because capital is a market, and markets are in constant evolution and constantly exposed to creative destruction, a notion to which Schumpeter was greatly devoted. For centuries Capitalism has done just that, evolve and improve with massive input via creative destruction. At times, our legislators have put up sensible guiderails. Mandates for bank reserves required for lending are the basis for sound banking. Accounting requirements for publicly traded companies have increased faith in the stock markets. Ending borrowing money on credit to purchase stock was a game changer, and for the best. Of course, government and business have made mistakes. The trajectory, though, is toward improvement.

Will there be some event, a Schumpeterian, creatively destructive approach that replaces Capitalism with a whole new economic tool kit? Maybe, but that day is likely centuries off. Why? For the foreseeable future, new ideas need capital for execution. Ideas need employees to build products and improve business processes. These have costs and to scale good ideas to great solutions, capital is needed or essential.

The need for capital to start and grow business may change sometime in the next few hundred years. There will be a time when the costs of energy and production for new ideas are costless, when machines can build anything, repair themselves, create and transform matter into goods, so the cost-of-living drops to zero. When that day arrives, a different kind of economics will be required because ideas will not need capital and citizens may not need income to live. Until then, Socialism is a poor replacement.

Conclusions

Back to Cordero for another insight: "The purpose of government is to make everyone's life better." The question delivered to both Socialist and Capitalists is, "*How?*".

Candidates running for office have used 'improvement' as an arrow in their quiver of objectives for good governance, but their execution has been terrible. Wouldn't it be nice to hear a politician state which policies did not work, why they didn't work, and then recommend new, innovative policies that deliver on our objective 'to make everyone's life better?' Most of us know how to make our own lives better. A slight refinement of Cordero's statement might be, "the foremost purpose of government is to make sure everyone can help themselves, especially the Forgotten Man, the person not afforded an excellent education from government which led to a life of poor jobs and the diminishment of family formation." Give everyone the same success tools and then government, get the hell out of the way.

'Making everyone's life better' has traditionally meant sending government checks as if better meant more money. Better is a value assessment more perfectly suggesting an improvement of one's life. Webster's defines value as, "of a more excellent or effective type or quality." A person getting a check is not smarter, does not have improved job skills or better social skills to operate within society. Money, the Socialist's approach to income problems, does not ameliorate the problems of diminished human capital. Money can't 'buy love' nor does it buy happiness, its pursuit of which is an essential natural right designated in the Declaration of Independence. Oddly, the focus of the Socialist approach has been on the redistribution of income, making money the focus of social revolution, something one might think would be the focus of Capitalists and their supposed focus on the acquisition of money as central to success. Both perspectives, though, fail to deliver on maximizing human capital as the central value proposition for governance.

Whereas Democratic Capitalism has attempted to introduce more options for failing schools and maximizing job creation through ideas and investment, Socialism and the Socialist approach have simply touted redistribution. The most basic requirement to assure economic equity and access to opportunity isn't money. The primary building block is a quality education. The Socialist, one-size-fits-all education provides a quality education to only one-third of our children. Equality of opportunity, or pay, or our pursuit of happiness begins with an education. It is the starter kit for the economic, social and cultural success sequence. If the Socialists in our midst would simply allow for a public education to have numerous education options from which parents can choose, this flexibility could provide access to parents to test the options available and find the highest quality solution for their children.

This book has repeatedly returned to education, so apologies are in order for the repetition. In fairness to the repetition, though, freedom is the cornerstone of greatness in any nation's road to success. Without a great education for every citizen, our freedom has diminished and Democracy fails. Good intentions surrounding education attainment are not good enough. Great results must be a mandate, and not just for education.

Schumpeter suggested that the integration of the two philosophies would be unlikely because of their broad divergence in execution. This is both true and false. True, because when mixing the Socialist approach with democratic Capitalism, our government has failed the average American if only because every two, four or eight years, we flop from one approach to the other, getting nowhere. America has not figured out how to integrate both into a single strategy.

The Chinese have integrated a sliver of Capitalism with Socialism, with defined limits for success. The Chinese have had much economic success integrating some property rights in their Constitution while significantly limiting the costs of social monopolies.

America has a similar task of integration of Socialist and Capitalist ideologies. Our twenty-first challenge is that a Socialist approach is occasionally required to deliver assistance to those in need who cannot provide for themselves. The question for advocates of both styles of government is, *How much is too much? How much is Just Right?* And how to change when intentions and results are at odds. As Goldilocks is not available to test the governmental porridge, there is a solution, but it is not set in concrete as our government is today.

Our national challenge is to understand who and when each approach is required; then—like scientists—we much test and validate results constantly to assure great results personally, corporately, and nationally.

CHALLENGES TO GREAT GOVERNMENT, AND A FIX!

AMERICA HAS REINVENTED ITSELF REPEATEDLY since 1776. We are always between utter destruction and the beckoning light on the hill. The Revolutionary and Civil Wars presented the greatest schisms and broadest changes since its founding. Political warfare, though, has been a constant since the entrance of political parties in the late 1890s. This century we have returned to the convulsive anger of the first political factions, the Anti-Federalists and Federalists, with Democrats and Republicans angrily divergent about almost any policy and fully divergent on political principles of governance, a strong nationalist versus the founding principles of a limited federal government. Confronted with the acceleration of big money into politics, media alignment by political party, and the intolerant megaphone of the Internet, America is remaking itself again. Perhaps, though, we are not changing in a healthy manner as there seems to be no exit from the anger. The path forward, promoted by our leaders, has meant more intolerance, more elitism, and more money. Going down this path returns us to an infamous statement by a very insightful friend, Cordero Holmes. "American government is looking more and more like Crazy King George." Crazy indeed. Our politics is so partisan, government without common sense seems the norm.

Mr. Holmes is not a political wonk, just an average young man who understands his success begins with himself and is not dependent on King George or any current Washington wannabees, and they are numerous. The voters should be worried, and they are to some extent. Gallup tests our perspective by polling Right Way, Wrong Direction for the last decades, and Wrong Way has with near uniformity polled over 60 percent.

After the Constitutional Convention which erected a limited federal government, two political factions brewed at the center of politics, one favoring a stronger central government, the other a republic of free men that elected their leaders as organized during the convention. The former produced ideas like The Sedition Act of 1798 during John Adams administration that jailed and fined persons who spoke against President Adams. Alexander Hamilton, the leader of the stronger central government faction, was disappointed in the Constitution if only because he wanted a much stronger government, more of a constitutional monarchy where federal elites could veto state laws among other ideas. Thomas Jefferson, the leader of the faction seeking more distribution of power to the states and citizens, followed Adams as the president helped repeal the Sedition Act and put America on a century-long tenure where a limited federal government won the day. America averted a retreat to a national government though Jefferson would become a strong executive, especially with the Louisiana Purchase, which was the largest one-time expansion of America; there was also an invasion of congressional responsibilities for spending. The fight for a strong central government, a more autocratic government, though, is back this century and last, with Democrats preaching a very centralized, autocratic approach versus the limited federal government design averred by Jefferson and Madison at the Convention.

Regardless, for 240 years America, has transited through many challenging times. The ability of the voter to our change our path with new Independent leaders is essential for a clear path for our future, a path defined not by elites and the rich (and Crazy King George) but of their own common sense pulled along as a collection of our common humanity and values, not a collective.

Citizens get the impression that government today is out of sync with common sense if only because of their growing distrust of government. Our new nobility in media, politics and the academy are populated more than ever by the overly educated, well-to-do, power seekers who have their eyes on the past, on the status quo that protects their treasure and power. As their power increases, the good outcomes for the rest of us are not on their radar. Government leads with partisanship, not by financial or social results. Unless the citizen is part of a favored group, they are off the political radar.

Spin rules.

Marketing insinuation rules.

Divided media narratives rule.

Spending rules instead of results.

Critical thinking is out the back door.

Evidence-based governance is a contradiction of terms.

America is fumbling along with 'adequate' as an objective, protecting partisan power.

Socialists propose more government spending and more programs while Conservatives propose a limited government, but with lots of spending, too.

Americans know something is wrong because 60 percent think neither party represents them. Even the political parties know something is amiss. They understand the voters' dissatisfaction. Tag lines for the presidential campaigns respond to voters' desire for better governance. 'Make America Great Again,' and 'Build Back Better' ring true to the voter. Something needs to be done. Much is askew. The execution of each party, though, has been terrible. Election slogans have not translated into actionable insights for improved leadership. Our government is not just poorly run; it spends huge volumes of money on solutions that do not meet intended objectives. No results or poor results are hurting everyone. The more responsibilities the government takes on, the less productive Americans become.

Government should be run like every other organization in existence, by measuring results against stated objectives. Businesses evaluate their success (as do their customers) on evidence regarding meeting goals for success including the quality and price of their products. So, too, do nonprofits and religious organizations. When revenues dip or expenses increase, something must be done to rectify the situation. If a CFO invests in plant and equipment accepting a 75 percent return on that investment and only a 10 percent is obtained, that CFO is in trouble. If a CEO tells Wall Street that growth will be 6 percent next quarter and revenue is flat, the stock tanks and the CEO is in the hotseat. Congress is America's chief financial officer, and they seem not to care a whit whether spending produces good financial, social, or cultural results. Their only objective is producing political results: more power and more money.

When a government program does not meet objectives, the result is spun in a way that makes the result look good, or, barring success, a request for more money is made. Billions are spent during elections in which one party tells us how good they are and how bad the other party is, and vice versa. Who are we to believe? Both parties are telling the truth. The other party is terrible, and that includes both parties.

When poverty in America is flat for sixty-five years despite spending upwards of $40 trillion dollars, no one blinks. No one takes responsibility. Ditto for the decline in education proficiency. What about the $100 trillion in underfunding for our retirement system? These are huge problems, bigger than any heard about during elections and they are driving our nation to mediocrity. But no one mentions them as a priority.

Neither politicians nor their appointed bureaucrats are accountable for inadequate or poor results. Few bureaucrats are fired for low performance. Few politicians lose elections because of their stewardship of poorly performing programs. And citizens cannot sue for their money back when the government does not perform. Without accountability, without an institution in government that is responsible for transparent reporting of the financial and social efficacy of policies and programs, the voter is held hostage to the preferred method of communications from Washington: spin and insinuation.

How do we get from an angry, intolerant, set of Crazy Kings, to a government of leaders focused on evidence and outcomes?

The Scientific Method Can Help with Great Governance

Good leaders promote objectives and track evidence to assure those objectives are met. Great leaders *exceed* objectives. This is not unlike science. When evidence supports the hypothesis, the objective is met resulting in good news to the science community, a validated discovery. Markets and the businesses in markets act similarly. When the hypothesis does not work as stated, things change. Our personal lives align with the scientific method as well, as we seldom repeat an error in judgment. Einstein put this human habit in perspective: "Insanity is doing the same thing over and over and expecting different results." Stating and meeting objectives is a value habit. It's a way of life for all of us. Failure is possible but translates into more theories and more testing. Scientists are in a constant race to find the truth. Our legislators and political executives should take note. Incorporating a mandate for stating objectives and meeting or exceeding those objectives is essential for great political leadership, a path for leaders to incorporate virtue, good leadership and good decision-making into the institutions of government. Unfortunately, Einstein's insanity rule predominates.

Over the last four months, from December 2020 to April 2021, two COVID-related bills have been introduced and passed into law: the $900 billion December COVID Relief and Stimulus under Trump, $1.9 trillion Stimulus and Relief under Biden. In neither of the two stimulus bills is there any measure of expected results. Nothing from the mouths of our leaders about the expected effects of the spending. Nada in the press. No Keynesian averred the benefits of how borrowed money can create demand, side economic growth, and job formation. Silence. If we are spending money to create economic growth during a year of already spectacular economic recovery, then shouldn't the voter be told of the expected benefit or if no benefit, the liability? The cost of the three sets of stimulus checks to individuals and families total $867 billion dollars. What effect was expected and what occurred? Keynesians love to stimulate a slow economy during a recession, so the first check in April 2020 made sense as economic growth declined 33 percent in Q2 2020. The second and third stimulus checks came during America's fastest expansion in decades—31 percent in Q3 2020, 4.5 percent in Q4 2020, and 6.4 percent in Q1 2021. As counter intuitive, stimulus checks went to 127 million people, but only 8.1 million were unemployed and in need of assistance. The Federal Reserve has not published results. The National Bureau of Economic Research—nothing. The Congressional Budget Office. Nothing. Our political leaders. Nothing. And why were we sending checks to people that were gainfully employed? Should the focus instead be on those in need? One might speculate the spending binges were more about getting votes than promoting sound economic policy. The result from the spending was heavy spending on the demand side of the economy, especially on consumer products, that has created supply side havoc and inflation. Even the Keynesians in our midst should have provided warnings, but few if any arrived.

Regarding the $2.3 trillion quasi-infrastructure bill that eventually was slimmed to $1.a trillion is spending that is not what one would traditionally think of as infrastructure; there is no discussion of what any of the numerous spending initiatives affect and consequences or benefits. Certainly, repairing roads and bridges is especially important, but why hasn't the federal and state governments maintained our roads in the past? Why have we waited to repair them instead of repairing them as the need arose? Americans accept that any level of spending is fine but there must be a benefit for spending, or the dollars are wasted. Americans need evidence that Washington's will to spend is matched by *evidence* that spending produces results and benefits for us all. More important, if our government has been a poor steward of repairing our roads for the last 30 years, perhaps the Federal Gas Tax should just be returned to the states so we can figure our priorities locally. Why is critical information hard to come by? Why isn't the press more skeptical, more inquisitive about how our money is spent? Perhaps a course or two in experimental sciences would push their boundaries.

This is not to say that we need to elect scientists. They can be as political as politicians. The institutions of government, however, the political infrastructure upon which policy and programs are created and the processes upon which legislation is built, must be evidence-based, like the scientific method, like markets and businesses, and like our personal lives. In Washington, evidence-based thinking, critical thinking, is routinely replaced by statistical spin and Saul Alinsky (*Rules for Radicals)* propaganda. Worse, far too often spin is replaced by a very thin patina of honesty to mask outright lies. Political marketing and commentary are the best Madison Avenue marketing one can buy. Great marketing must be followed by great governance which, sadly, is routinely ignored.

Critical thinking is in truly short supply in Washington D.C. Painting oneself as a candidate that 'follows the science' has been a common refrain used to convey right-mindedness, never mind that speaker of these words have little if any understanding of what science or the process of discovery is. Candidates are great at political science, which is a misnomer when associated with a policy and a program because the science is only applied to marketing, polling, focus group testing, and spin to assure reelection, not the efficacy of the policy outcome and good governance.

Good scientific reasoning should be the elixir for great guidance. It should also be the guidepost for voters to determine what ideas meet objectives and which do not because evidence is available and easily visible for voters to discern. Except no national scoreboard exists. Media seldom provides both sides of the political story which would help readers score the effectiveness of ideas. There is no single source of the truth, no go-to agency, no third eye of politics, and no public-facing debate of ideas. The voter is left on his own to navigate vast pools of biased information to get some sense of the truth. Few of us have the time to do what the press was incredibly good at sixty years ago—orchestrating the symphony of data to provide some sense of the insensible. Walter Cronkite, Tom Brokaw and Harry Reasoner stand out as beacons of news wisdom. During their tenure, the political parties were not so philosophically divided which made being even-handed easier. In the confusion of twenty-first century narratives, when great commentators are needed to cut through the fog, these great personalities have no replacements. And their wisdom is sorely needed. Some source of sensibility is needed for our votes to be something more than a result of marketing-generated anger.

Good governance also requires that untested ideas pass a sniff test. This is propensity valuation, whether an idea has enough merit to test. Propensity valuation is something we all do, including scientists. Before we state an opinion, we ruminate whether it is appropriate given whom we are talking to. When we buy something, we cogitate whether the investment is equivalent to the benefit. A politician should ponder whether some basic math scratching on the back on a notepad produces numbers that add up to something worth testing. For instance, Medicare for All resonated for many on the Left because it met a *political* sniff test. It sounded *great*. Applying budgetary sniffing to the idea provided, however, more than a few challenges to its potential efficacy as the costs were large and the end of private insurance was unwelcome to many. The economic sniff test is all too often a missed step.

Political communications with citizens run the gamut across a sea of soft sciences like economics, sociology, psychology, and politics. Soft sciences are not like hard sciences that produce hypotheses that are either true or false, like Newton's Three Laws of Motion or Einstein's Theory of Relativity. Soft sciences produce multiple outputs that run the gamut from great results to awful, to policy that sometimes seems to work well and sometimes poorly, and a panoply of possible outputs in the middle. For instance, tax cuts with near uniformity produce both economic growth and increased or neutral tax revenues. In a small minority of cases, tax cuts may produce no growth and negative tax revenue. A division of evidence occurs in opinion pages: The *Wall Street Journal* will uniformly promote tax cuts whereas the *New York Times* recently stated that "Tax Cuts Never Work." Who is the voter to believe? Because the rate of return for tax cuts varies widely, any proposal could be spun as acceptable or unacceptable.

The 2017 business and individual tax cuts were rated by the Congressional Budget Office as a $2 trillion cut for businesses. The CBO uses a straight-line method for its estimate. That is, if business gets a 10 percent tax cut, revenues will drop by 10 percent. Simple math. Dynamic scoring, which takes into account the expected increase in economic output and thus increased tax revenues was not used. Had America erected a dashboard, one would have found that the cuts produced something quite different. While business tax revenues were down about $100 billion (not $2 trillion), individual taxes rose because of higher employment and wages and thus increased personal tax revenues, producing record tax collections for the treasury. Depending on where one gets their news, this was the greatest tax cut ever or a nightmare that put America more in debt. Of course, neither is true. The real golden nugget is that 70 percent of the business tax reductions wound up in the pockets of The Forgotten Man via a job and increased income. The bottom two quintiles of income earners had the greatest increase in income, exceeding wage increases of the middle class and the top earners. The question for voters should be, "How do we do this again to help the little guy?"

Though most of us do not trust government, we habitually seek a big solution. Literally, any solution sounds good. We are looking for big ideas from Washington despite our distrust of government. We want to hear about how government will improve our lives and how it will invest in our future and our children's future. The challenge is understanding how spending just to spend dollars differs from investing to improve our productivity. In a question-and-answer session during the Democrat presidential primaries, when asked about the costs of her extensive social program recommendations, Kamala Harris said that these were all investments and so the costs did not matter because they all had payback. I am sure, as a collection of people who invest our precious dollars regularly and wisely, we all leaned in. What she failed to appreciate, as we natively understand, is that paybacks can be negative, zero, small, medium, or great. Too often, the political sniff test passes whereas the actual financial sniff does not.

Government should only make investments that produce great paybacks; otherwise the dollars are investments that reduce our economic productivity. Sadly, the proclivity of both parties is to spend regardless of benefit; the amount of dollars spent is more important than financial or social outcomes.

Even good solutions have another propensity problem. Competing variables can be mitigated or enhanced by other variables that are at play. Do tax cuts generally increase worker take home pay and induce a degree of economic growth that is proportional to the size of the tax cut? Yes. Numerous contending economic variables can diminish the value of the tax cut: increased regulation, decreased trade and immigration, an increasing Federal Reserve Rate, and a host of other variables. Tax increases during the Clinton administration accompanied a rising economy. This is often used as an example for increasing taxes. Were the tax increases the cause of rising GDP or was it the Internet revolution, increased private investment and reduction of regulation and the size of government under Clinton's (*"the era of big government is over"*) guidance? Although a white paper may have been done to examine all four variables, good luck to the voter on finding the study. For the voter trying to make sense of tax cuts or tax increases, he/she should ask whether more or less dollars in the paycheck is a good idea.

An American Success Dashboard would be an enormous benefit. CEOs and CFOs have analytics at their fingertips so they can understand the effects of their decisions on company performance. The political will to provide the same level of decision support in government is nil, if only because it would display the enormity of incompetence in Washington. How to get from spin to well-visualized information requires a change in culture in Washington. To reset American governance, a new way to govern is required: evidence-based government. Though the tools a CFO is using to judge corporate performance is a great example of good corporate government, science provides an underlying foundation for evidence-based governance.

Streven's *The Knowledge Machine* provides great instruction about how science and scientists have approached the Scientific Method. His guidance would be well taken by politicians and voters alike. Streven's cautions us that science is not a one-and-done endeavor but a lengthy, evolutionary process where one set of ideas about a subject changes over time to a new understanding of a problem, a new paradigm. The scientific community's discovery process is political, subjective, and emotional outside the laboratory, not unlike politics, but inside the lab, science lives by the Iron Rule of science. *The Iron Rule:*

1) Strive to settle all arguments by empirical testing.

2) Conduct an empirical test to decide between a pair of hypotheses; perform an experiment or measurement so that one of whose possible outcomes can be explained by one hypothesis (and accompanying cohort) but not the other.

These two bullets are the unwavering basis of the scientific method, which was given to us by Francis Bacon 400 years ago and which launched the scientific revolution persisting today. Applying this approach to our everyday lives is the essence of critical thinking. Applying the Iron Rule to business, religious and nonprofit institutions, and government is common sense. The Iron Rule is also the format we use in our daily decisions. The items we buy are a test between two or three or many choices of product. We choose one. If it meets our hypothesis of good value and good price, we buy the product again. If the hypothesis fails, we move on to another produce.

The Iron Rule, which with near uniformity is embraced by scientists, by the citizens, small business, entrepreneurs, and every publicly traded business, is summarily ignored by politicians. Though huge volumes of data and evidence are produced and stored by government, statistical political spin is favored over actionable intelligence, compromising good (or great) governance.

Below is a chart of the scientific method from the website *Sutori*. The method is a repeating process that never stops because new information creates new options for discovery. Scientific discovery is self-healing, always improving as new data requires new experimentation and new conclusions. From scientists to grocery shoppers, this straightforward thinking is daily fare.

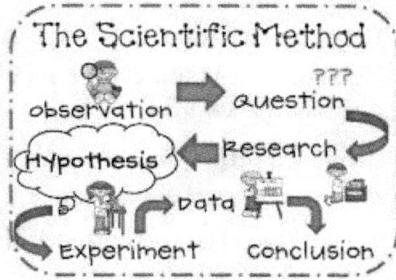

Illustration of the Scientific Method

Simply enough? It took a few thousand years for civilization to reach the guts of Bacon's 1620 proposal: If testing your hypothesis does not match observations, find a new hypothesis. There is also a falsifiable component to the method, which is if your theory is shown to be false, even in a single case, the hypothesis is invalid. Bacon's method is the essence of sound reasoning and critical thinking. The cornerstone of the method requires adherence to collection and the quality of data collection. Some theories take decades or centuries to resolve if only because quality data is hard to come by and the devices to collect data may be lacking. The collection of observational empirical data is extremely hard work and perhaps a reason why most of us shy away from the profession. As important is the fact that theories that seem to work in one century can be undone by new observations because the tools to collect data radically improve the quality of the data. Newton did not have measurement tools to confirm the theory of a curvy universe proposed by Einstein. Nor did Einstein have the tools to measure galactic spin that showed his theory of gravity had a new variable to consider—dark matter.

The same challenges await a more scientific approach to governance. Good governance requires constant attention to information about the results of government programs which—when programs are not working according to their original hypothesis—need to evolve.

If there is a single conundrum for government, it is that politicians and bureaucrats spend their time attempting to prove the approach true, rather than coming to accept that the data has falsified their original proposition. Information is routinely ignored in favor of marketing that sounds good. It is embarrassing. Because politicians are not accountable like CEOs and CFOs, they cannot be fired for their lack of results, their poor stewardship. They can overcome poor performance by masking their failures with big money contributions to fund marketing that makes failure seem like success.

The Iron Rule for Governance differs slightly from the Iron Rule of Science. For governance, the Iron Rule should produce *Best Practices* rather than a theory of everything. Is there a single format that works for educating all our children? Probably not. The reason federalism, which accommodates the needs of fifty different states, is this: What may work well in one state may not work in another. The Governance Iron Rule mimics economic markets where multiple quality solutions exist and poor solutions go extinct. Evolution of working ideas that evolve from good to great results assure that governance continually improves.

The Iron Rule of Government:

1) A hypothesis is proposed and prioritized as important and in need of a solution;

2) Measurable metrics for success are clearly defined;

3) Debate and data produce a variety of test approaches, and states are used as test beds;

4) Best Practices that meet objectives evolve as data collection continues; good solutions may be improved upon; bad solutions are removed, updated, or transformed;

5) Continual testing provides feedback for continual improvement and a menu of best practices, or exit from strategies that fail;

6) When programs fail to meet objectives, new hypotheses are generated, and the process restarts.

The Socialist approach assumes there is a single solution and often when the solution works poorly, outcomes are touted as satisfactory or good. Extending the Socialist, one-size-fits-all strategy, most federal and state programs are immortal. Once built, they are forever stuck in time. Even in hard sciences, like physics and engineering, which tout discrete solutions, scientists understand that the discovery process is evolutionary as new data expands the requirement for more discovery. Science evolves over time, continually improving its theories.

Socialism expands over time without improving its original hypothesis.

Science is a continual improvement process that Feynman described earlier as failure after failure which hopefully leads to success. Thomas Edison provides a famous example of the ardor required for science—the invention of the light bulb. The process required 1,000 attempts to finally get a solution that worked. When asked about the sizeable number of failures, he responded, "I didn't fail 1,000 times. The light bulb was an invention with 1,000 steps." Each step improved his original hypothesis. And thousands of more steps have led other inventors to improve the incandescent light bulb and invent other bulbs like florescent, neon, and LED. And we are still inventing. For policy and program to have long-term success, leaders must invest in evidence-based discovery for ways to improve solutions that have the greatest efficacy, and leaders must dispatch those that have failed.

Updating Legislative and Executive Culture

Testing is not part of political science or public policy creation. If political science is to have any chance of producing twenty-first century, national success, it must adopt testing as a crucial political component. Testing is not part of our legislative process or an institution of governance. French enlightenment philosopher Baron de Montesquieu, who wrote of the importance of separation of powers between branches of government, a key component of American government, made an especially important observation about institutions: "At the birth of societies, the leaders of republics create the institutions; thereafter, it is the institutions that form the leaders of republics." When acquisition of power is the primary institutional objective, testing and quality improvement are shoved ruthlessly to the side in favor of partisan, non-evidence-based leadership.

To insert testing in public policy formation, an institution is essential to monitor the evolution to twenty-first century governance. Like the Federal Reserve's dual mandate for employment and inflation, an Office of Innovations should have a quadruple mandate: simplicity, innovation, and testing, append-ed by visual intelligence to serve as a national dashboard of programs' suc-cesses and failures. As a best practice, these even mandates should be tested to validate their value.

First, simplicity is essential for any well-run organization whether busi-ness, nonprofit or government. Occam's Razor should be obeyed as great solutions are seldom if ever complex. If the new idea is not simple in concept and execution, move on. As noted earlier, complexity is a huge cost for large business organizations as well as our federal government, which is the largest organization in the history of the world. Simplicity is also a crucial factor for reviewing America's aging solutions. The review process is not unlike Edward Deming's Quality Process Improvement adopted by Japanese car makers in the 1960s. Using the Deming process encouraged continuous input from shop floor workers to the CEO and assured the best possible manufac-ture of the vehicle—whose quality always improved. The same approach is needed for America to create great outcomes from our government. Political processes have nullified quality improvements in government because they are more about continuous increases in partisan power, not an increasingly well-run government.

Second, innovation in business, society and culture is essential to American twenty-first century success, and so national policy must foster in-novation. Even more important, innovation *must* be a priority for government itself. Our government's administrative processes and infrastructure are aged. National needs are not prioritized, so everything is a priority, and nothing is a priority. Objectives are not set for government programs, so spending in-creases unabated.

Third, America has no national objectives nor a rating system to eval-uate individual responsibilities of government. Should our goal be to grow the economy 5 percent or 2 percent? Should we rate growth? Is two percent growth a 'D,' and is 2.5 percent an 'A.' Probably not, especially as America needs to grow more than 4 percent to compete with China. What should be in our list of priorities: the unemployment rate, inflation, taxation, and others. How about measuring the effects of any policy on The Forgotten Man? As objectives have never been on the radar of any politician or wonk, the voter is in the dark and our politics are on autopilot driven by big money, not an individual or national success.

Fourth, government information technology is so old that actionable information that should be available to government and citizen alike, *is dark, hidden, and difficult to find.* Information Technology problems do not need small tweaks; they need innovative transformations for America to be competitive internationally. Citizens and politicos are unable to decide what is working and what is not working because there is no transparent platform to view performance data; there is no measure of success or failure, only how much was spent! Even when benchmarks for success are proposed and not met, they are ignored. As stated earlier, a national scoreboard is an essential component for great governance.

Big Money and Leadership Problem

Political pandering regarding Obamacare that recommends its continuance and expansion is not good governance; yet this is precisely the approach our federal government employed for one hundred years for every public endeavor. First, create a Big Bang solution; then when it doesn't work, defend the poor results as good; then pretend the solution is the best thing since sliced bread and expand it to a broader audience.

A little honesty and virtue would be helpful. Virtue sadly has been replaced by the intellectual conceit that intelligence and good intentions beat common sense and good results.

How does American governance transition from politics based on consumption of power to leadership based on critical thinking?

Sadly, both Socialists and Capitalists love big, political money as well as foisting power over their minions funded by big money from business, unions, special interests, and very rich persons. Their interests are in protecting their treasures, whether their wealth, their point of view, or expanding their political power, all while devouring the needs of the citizen. Political enrichment at the expense of good problem solving is killing America. Only a change of habit in the voter will alter this. The voter needs new options and a new menu of political parties. New political innovation may be the elixir that remedies our nightmarish political challenge.

How to govern better is straight forward. Evidence-based government will help. Institutionalizing simplicity, government innovation and testing will help. These steps are an enhancement of federalism, a Federalism 2.0, if you will. As federalism is built on distributing power to the states, becoming test beds for new ideas, a menu of solutions for any problem should be a matter of routine federal governance. This approach can be driven down to the smallest of government entities, to counties, cities, townships, school districts and more. Even more important, testing becomes a pathway for Deming's Quality Improvement Process which engages feedback all the way down to the lowest level of feedback, the worker in business, the citizen for government, to fix problems when they arise. This allows governance to improve unceasingly.

Twenty-First Century Leadership

Numerous leadership tomes have been published, so repacking these lofty publications will not occur on these pages. What is evident in the lack of voters' trust is that few if any candidates match the pre-election promises in campaign commercials with the after-election execution of their duties. Much of this divergence comes from partisanship between the parties and the political power wielded by party leaders when it comes time to vote for a bill.

Were politicians able to take a No Big Money Pledge, this problem would evaporate as monied interests would have no political home. But do not expect many takers for small-donation-only campaigns. Candidates extoll their small donations, but big money drives speech and small money keeps the lights on in remote district offices. Ultimately, big money leads to ever increasing partisanship and a disconnect with the voter who is seeking candidates in the center.

Since the money challenge is unlikely to suddenly diminish, what character traits should the voter look for that lend to improved leadership? Humility, restraint, common sense, simplicity and virtue.

Harry Truman may be the most unknown of our twentieth century presidents, but he was a wonderful example of the traits needed to lead a nation, as he did, or a squad of soldiers, which he did in World War One. In just five quotes, he exemplifies all five qualities.

"It is amazing what you can accomplish if you do not care who gets the credit."

"America was not built on fear. America was built on courage, on imagination and an unbeatable determination to do the job at hand."

"The buck stops here."

"I never did give anybody hell. I just told the truth and they thought it was hell."

"In periods where there is no leadership, society stands still. Progress occurs when courageous, skillful leaders seize the opportunity to change things for the better."

Harry, and if you don't mind, I will call him Harry as I think he might prefer the common to the titled persona of president, entered early adulthood failing at farming and numerous business ventures. He then entered politics, via Tom Prendergast and the Kansas City political machine as a county judge. Though the position traditionally created wealth for judges via graft, Harry would never make a penny outside his salary. The steps from judge to congressman, to senator, to vice president, then president were always prefaced with a rejection of the promotion saying he was not qualified for the position.

His humility and the industriousness he learned as a farmer lent well to his on-the-job training.

Common sense and virtue meant he entered politics poor and left poor. During a senate campaign he slept in his car between events because there were no dollars in the campaign fund and none in his checking account. It was not about the money. This humble approach to life and to politics is not only endearing, it's the basis of good leadership.

William F. Buckley Jr. recommended, "I would rather be governed by the first 2,000 people in the Boston telephone directory than by the 2,000 people on the faculty of Harvard University." Having to build oneself up from lesser beginnings, to create something from little provides a vastly more complete person than someone whose high intelligence provides fast access to the academy's ivory towers or new high-tech business without sweat and toil and scraping by.

As common sense seemed routine during Harry's administration, it has gone missing this century. So too has humility. Restraint in government is a foreign concept. Yet all these qualities are essential in good (and perhaps, someday, great) governance.

166 | CAPITALISM, SOCIALISM, AND DEMOCRACY

Conclusion

If America is to compete with China and win the competition, the first step to success is to transform the federal government into a best run enterprise. The Socialist approach federal programs that now account for over 80 percent of the federal budget—in 1960 the percentage was 22 percent—has not achieved the results originally proposed. To restate three profoundly serious problems: Our retirement system is underfunded by at least $50 trillion (if not $100 trillion by my estimates); two-thirds of students do not reach adulthood with proficiency in key subjects required for twenty-first century jobs, and our War on Poverty has not reduced poverty an iota in its sixty years of existence. Transformative updates that delivered great outcomes could deliver $1.5 trillion dollars back to more productive uses vastly increasing economic growth. Each transformation requires a more scientific, a more marketlike, approach versus the current Socialist, one-size-fits-all method.

WHAT'S THE PLAN?

AMERICA HAS NEVER HAD A plan because it never needed one. We were competing with economies that were much smaller than ours, so we collaborated with competing nations to set up international frameworks for accounting, trade and defense which were good for all. When at war or at least significant odds with nations that did not share our framework, interactions have been minor since WWII. Trade with nations like the USSR, Red China, Cuba, and other non-western nations were limited, but as USSR became Russia and Red China, China lined with a bit of Capitalist green, and trade improved the lives of their countrymen. When China showed interest in both Capitalism and trade, the west jumped right in believing that economic success would be followed by more political freedom. This has not happened, and China's aim is to use their new wealth to demote America and the West from their leadership positions.

To build a plan to defend the western way of life, America needs a measurable objective, a strategy, and a set of tactics to meet the strategic aim and our goals. This is what Lute Olsen and every accomplished coach does. This is what every high performing business does. This is what every high performing person does. That no leader in either party has stepped forward with a strategic plan with a central goal to achieve is just short of total incompetence.

Economic growth in 2021 will be strong, between 6 percent and 8 percent, as the harsh decline from Coronavirus is replaced by the optimism of vaccinations opening our economy. Long-term economic growth projections devolve to an anemic 2 percent after full economic recovery in 2022. Most western nations will be envious of 2 percent as they will also return their pre-pandemic growth of well below two percent. As much of our stimulus payments went to purchase products manufactured in China, their growth will top 18 percent this year and likely be in the 6 percent range after 2022 and for the foreseeable future. With these two rates in mind, China will exceed our GDP by 2030 and double our GCP in another twenty years.

Were America to grow at 4.5 percent on average, China will not exceed our GDP at least through the end of the century and perhaps not ever given that their population will likely drop from 1.4 billion to 750 million during this century.

Challenges for China include:

- An aging demography and declining population.
- A centrally planned government with an increasingly heavy social policy that mitigates personal and business freedoms.
- Massive amounts of corruption, especially for state owned businesses rife with debt.

Challenges for America:

- **No common set of principles by which to govern:** Republicans and Democrats have irreconcilable differences about how to govern, so our leaders flop back and forth between two entirely different systems of governance, neither team moving the economic needle much past 2 percent while creating anger and resentment between parties and their voting blocks.

- **Poorly Performing Government Monopolies:** Vast swathes of government monopolies that are not meeting their financial or social objectives creating massive amount of borrowing for debts that will top 425 percent of GDP in seventy-five years (a huge and heavy anchor on economic growth.) Just two programs, Social Security and Medicare are underfunded $100 trillion with neither party producing a plan to fix the problem.

- **Laggard Education System:** Stagnation of individual and national human capital. The biggest shortcoming is a laggard education system that provides only a third of students with the proficiency required for twenty-first century jobs. In a century when technology and science jobs increase astronomically, a failing education system will be a huge drag on the economy.

- **Lack of focus on Innovation:** Creation of new ideas both commercially and for government

Is there a longer list for both nations? Yes. But that's another book. These are the biggest drivers of poor performance.

If our objective is to compete and beat China to protect our children's future—and it should be—then our parties need to agree on how to accomplish this goal and agree on a common set of principles by which we keep China at bay.

National Objective: To consistently grow the economy 4.5 percent annually for the next thirty years, if not through the end of the century, by focusing on growth for *the essential economic currencies* for economic success in this century—*ideas, innovation, and invention.*

Strategy: To create an evidence-based government with transformative programs to renovate poorly performing programs that have negative or neutral financial and social results. These include the retirement system, education, the War on Poverty, health care, and immigration. Each of these will require stimulating innovation in the private sector as well as government. Old thinking, the status quo, needs a place in history, not in our strategic plan for success.

Objective #1: Increase educational proficiency from 33 percent to 50 percent in fifteen years, and to 95 percent by 2100, with a stretch goal of 90 percent by 2075. Increased human capital is America's number one need and the largest drag on future growth and personal happiness.

Objective #2: Transform our retirement system from a tax-based to a savings-based system retaining a safety net for the poor and those in need; this will reduce retirement system costs by 75 percent over the next forty years and build $100 trillion in individual retirement nest eggs, increasing GDP an additional 1 percent to 2 percent annually.

Objective #3: Create a Chief Simplicity, Innovation and Results Reporting Office to work with the Congressional Budget Office to manage the results of each current and new public program, to constantly test and re-evaluate solutions, and to publish the results on a National Analytics Dashboard available to politicos and voters alike. Reduce government compliance costs by 50 percent over the next ten years by employing smarter, simpler regulation that plans for competition.

Objective #4: Increase public research funding for science and technology broadly, with focus on artificial intelligence, quantum computing, genomics (and related fields), the hard sciences, energy, space and any newly evolving twenty-first century industries. Secondly, prioritize immigration to attract entrepreneurs and innovators in these fields to maximize idea generation. Thirdly, incent private investment in these areas to further stimulate idea generation and job growth.

Objective #5: Get the political parties to agree. Getting them to agree on anything, even these four objectives, will not be easy, but the outcome will be an economy that can grow closer to four percent, perhaps higher, with a much more focused approach to innovation that is *the* essential variable for America success. This transformational approach will also give the political parties a common platform by which to lead and by which voters can decide for whom to vote. *Had the first four objectives been in place over the last ten years, the 2020 budget would have been $3.2 trillion dollars instead of $4.8 trillion, with much less borrowing and lower taxes!*

How Evidence-Based Government Could Work

The above plan is an abbreviated version of CIVIL Governance's broader strategic plan. CIVIL in a non-partisan think tank seeking independent solutions upon which both parties could agree. The foundation of CIVIL's mission is Performance before Politics. Put another way, for every dollar spent Americans should receive more than a dollar in value. Currently, have our tax dollars are not well spent. We pay twice our fair share in taxes. The above four objectives were chosen for this book because they provide the greatest economic growth and the biggest reductions in poverty. These examples are used here to help provide structure for how a Socialist approach, when necessary, can be structured to achieve great results by incorporating performance metrics, markets and competition.

How would evidence-based governance work? Two examples may help, education and retirement systems.

Education: Increasing Human Capital with Stellar Education

Historically, education has been a constitutional right owned by states. Federal oversight began in the 1960s with the creation of the US Department of Education during the Carter Administration. Ever since, working in unison, local, state, unions and federal initiatives are erected as top-down solutions with the intent to improve what was apparent in the 1960s, that inner city schools whose students were predominately persons of color were less than adequately educated. Solutions included Title IX creation and expansion, busing, equalization of per student spending, No Child Left Behind, creation of public-sector unions, increased funding and pay for teachers, and Common Core, to name a few. All these programs dedicated resources to the teach-side of education, presuming that top-down administration was the key to improving education. This approach very much aligns to the Socialist approach, that more governance must produce good government. It should be noted that both the Left and Conservative wonks bought into this approach. In the 1990s charters were introduced by Conservatives which provided a sliver of choice to a tiny minority of parents. Though there are examples of great success in Charters, notably Success Academy in New York, with near uniformity, none of these programs increased student education proficiency. In fact, average student proficiency is down this century as is America's education competence among industrialized nations.

Sixty years of non-performance is no longer acceptable. The evidence shows that employing the top-down, national policy does not address the learning side of education, the parent and the student. Without a better plan, our inability to educate our children will create a two-class society, the haves and have nots with the have nots becoming an increasingly large segment of our society which will begin to compete with android like robotics after mid-century, something we should do everything in our power to prevent.

Education is not only crucial to assure a well-governed, democratic nation, but education is essential for a growing, healthy economy. Additionally, a high-quality education is the primary building block for improved income and stable family formation which are key variables for happiness and personal economic success. In the twenty-first century, a quality education also translates into a better supply of new ideas and innovation. Better educated citizens in an open and free market will have a higher propensity to usher their ideas to market, improving incomes and wealth.

Our national challenge? Only about 1/3 of our students are proficient in key subjects that are essential for twenty-first century jobs, according to the National Assessment of Educational Progress. Key subjects include math, science, reading, writing and history. Students proficient in these subjects have the learning skills and knowledge base to complete a college curriculum or any post-secondary education. Students with high proficiency are crucial for our evolving economy because proficient students will be capable of performing well in the evolving technology and bioscience industries, where twenty-first century jobs will proliferate. Without increasing student competence, America will need to import more and more talent from abroad. Though a great immigration policy is essential to American success, increasing our own pool of human capital is our highest national important priority. Without a strategy to educate every budding citizen, a two-class society is assured. Because our efforts over the last sixty years have decreased student proficiency, we are in the midst of an evolving national emergency that creates much talk but zero execution. Evidence says we must change, but the political will to sustain the education monopoly is well funded and tone deaf.

Our #1 national goal should be to increase educational proficiency for all students. Does this hypothesis pass an evidence-based sniff test? Is there enough evidence to test this hypothesis? Even in the 1960s evidence was building. In 1965, Democrat Daniel Patrick Moynihan, hired by President Lyndon Johnson to develop policy for the War On Poverty, challenged this status quo thinking in the *Moynihan Report*. He wrote: "The steady expansion of welfare programs can be taken as a measure of the steady disintegration of the Negro family structure over the past generation in the United States." His voice was ignored by his party and the president. The opportunity to transform a failing school system fifty-five years ago vaporized into partisan politics and gigantic union political contributions that funded top-down initiatives that favored one-size-fits-all thinking. The harm created by a lack of education was supplemented by social theory that redistributed income as a poverty palliative. Moynihan was shut down by critics in his own party, if only because the power of money trumped critical thinking and evidence-based policy.

Today, the Internet makes quick work of a sniff test as well as much evidence that a check from government does not reduce poverty so much as renders it acceptable. Evidence also shows that an education is the first building block to prevent poverty. The following infographic contains information from the Bureau of Labor Statics, Statistica, Prison Policy, Daily Signal, and National Center for Health Services and was sniffed out online in about two hours.

Checking the available data is routinely ignored by pols in favor of expanding the current policy and paradigm even when the policy is not delivering on its stated objective. This cursory review recommends America has done an immense disservice not only to people of color but for most every student in a failing or underperforming school (approximated 65,000 of America's 131,000 schools.)

Numerous benefits result from acquiring a quality education and even more gains as education is added after high school. To name a few: increased lifetime income, lower crime rates, higher marriage rates, and lower imprisonment rates. For America to compete in the technology arena, we need more high competency among students to qualify for college, or college equivalent education solutions that will likely evolve in the twenty-first century. The following six charts were Googled in less than 2 hours and paint a view of how education affects personal and national economics. The challenge to our leaders is simple: with information so readily at hand, why isn't Education the top national priority.

The Effects of an Insufficient Education

The education gap in marriage continues to grow

% of U.S. adults ages 25 and older who are married, by education

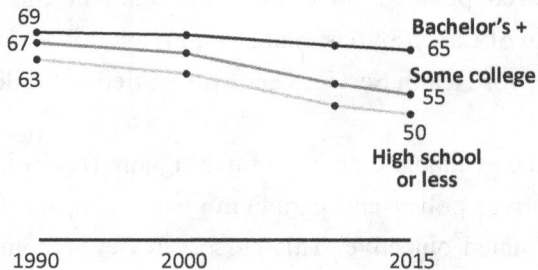

69
67
63

Bachelor's +
65

Some college
55

50

High school
or less

1990   2000   2015

Note: "Some college" includes those with an associate degree and those who attended college but did not obtain a degree. Adults who are separated are not classified as married.
Source: Pew Research Center analysis of 1990-2000 decennial censuses and the 2010 and 2015 American Community Surveys (IPUMS).

PEW RESEARCH CENTER

Poverty rate in the United States in 2020, by education

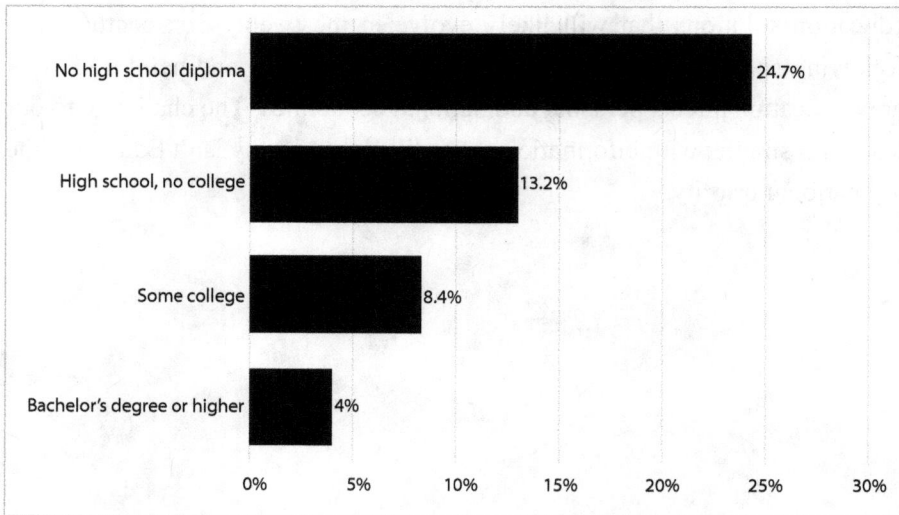

Education	Poverty rate
No high school diploma	24.7%
High school, no college	13.2%
Some college	8.4%
Bachelor's degree or higher	4%

0%   5%   10%   15%   20%   25%   30%

Source: Staistica

Median Weekly Income by Education

Median usual weekly earnings of full-time wage and salary workers age 25 years and older, by educational attainment, first quarter–third quarter 2019, not seasonally adjusted

- – – – Total, all educational levels
- —— Advanced degree
- – – Bachelor's degree only
- —— Some college or associate degree
- —— High School graduates, no college
- ······ Less than a high school diploma

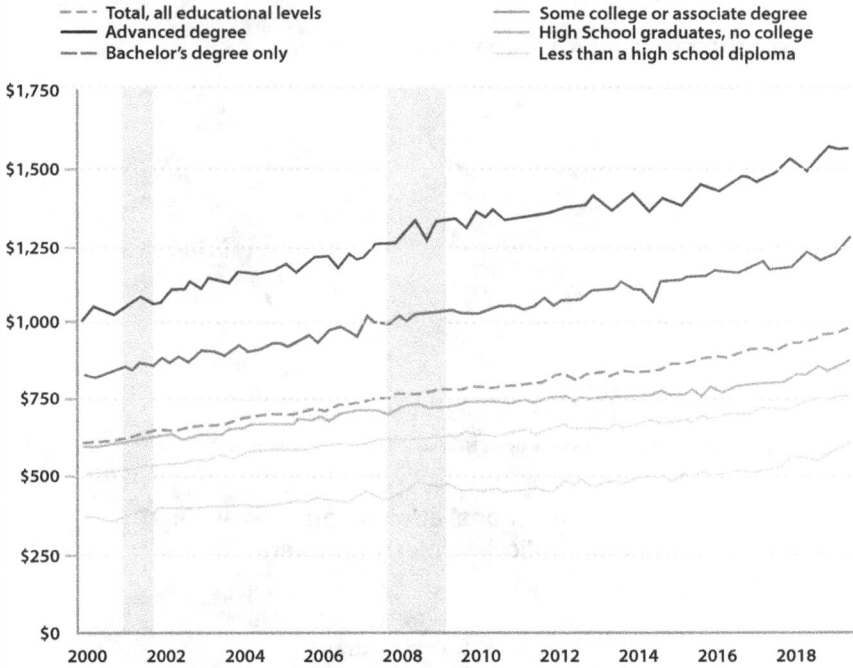

Shaded areas represent recessions as determined by the National Bureau of Economic Research.

Source: Bureau of Labor Statistics

Four in 10 Children are Born to Unwed Mothers

The percentage of children born outside of marriage has skyrocketed, with a six-fold increase since 1960. Currently, the figure is highest among black, but the rate of increase is highest among whites and Hispanics.

PERCENTAGE OF BIRTHS TO UNWED MOTHERS

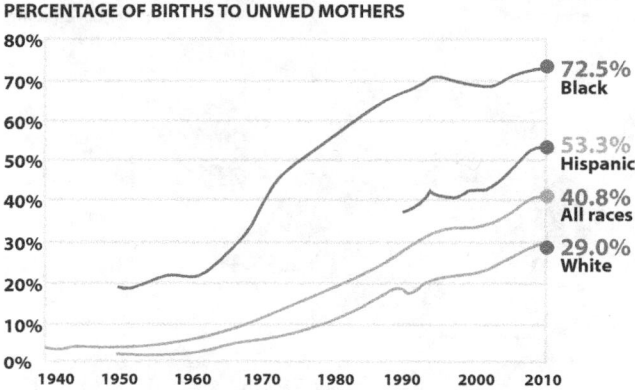

72.5% Black
53.3% Hispanic
40.8% All races
29.0% White

Source: National Center for Health Statistics. National Vital Statistics Reports, 2011

Educational attainment:
General public & formerly incarcerated

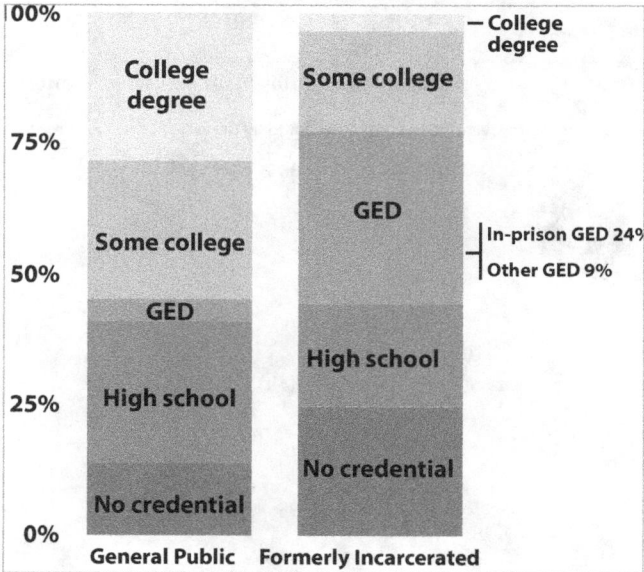

In-prison GED 24%
Other GED 9%

General Public   Formerly Incarcerated

Source: prisonpolicy.org

Poverty and Family

Percent of families with one or more members in the labor force for 27 weeks or more who lived below the poverty level in 2018

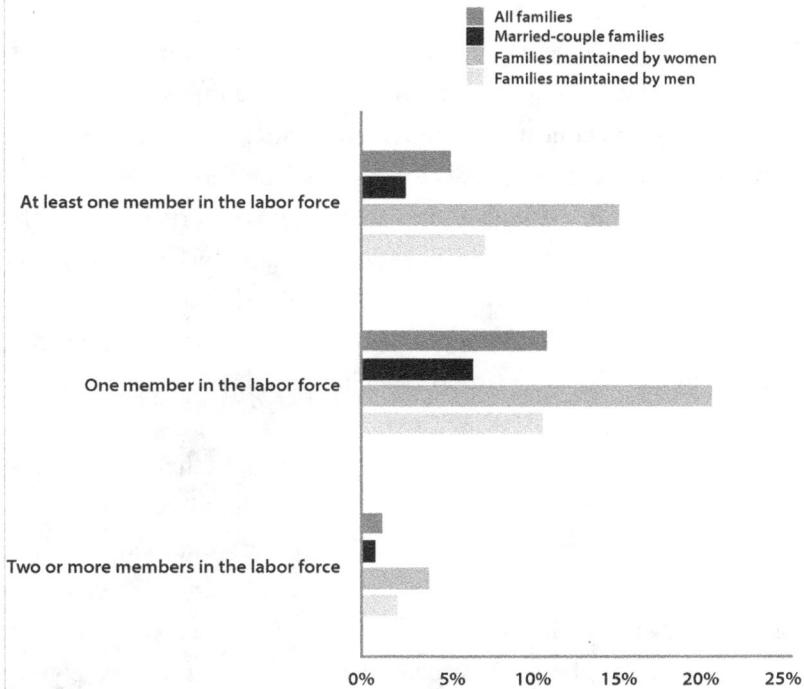

Source: Bureau of Labor Statistics

In the early decades of the twentieth century, the value of increasing education requirements from six years of schooling to twelve became apparent after World War II. More years of education not only provided enough additional subject matter proficiency for veterans to qualify for college under the GI Bill. Also, *IQs increased.* Conversely, a poor education can reduce a student's IQ, something that should never happen, but this occurs repeatedly in our inner cities and rural communities where obtaining a quality education is difficult. This is *education inequality at its worst* because richer suburban people can afford to send their children to competing schools when the public school is failing or underperforming. Fixing the poor performance of our failing and underperforming schools and income inequality, wealth inequality, and economic mobility are reduced, as evidenced by the above charts. Danny

Williams, a friend, and pickup basketball point guard extraordinaire, and arm-chair philosopher, put into words what many inner-city parents must think. This kind of inequality 'should be illegal.' He also added that our leaders need to show some 'common sense.' He is correct.

According to *Reason.com*, our average IQ increased thirty points last century, most of the increase likely occurring during the first six decades. In the 1960s and beyond, as education requirements flattened or devolved, our collective IQ suffered. Increases in education proficiency and IQ are a noticeably big deal during a century when another bump in IQ of thirty points is critical. America needs to duplicate early twentieth century successes if we are to retain our leadership in science and technology and increase our economic output. The new jobs of the twenty-first century will require higher IQs and greater education proficiencies. Increasing human education capital is the cornerstone of our future economic success.

An obvious benefit of a quality education, a benefit that government policy makers have ignored for decades, is that with improved education proficiency, fewer and fewer people will feed into our welfare system. Put another way, education is the key tool in our War on Poverty, one that has been long disregarded. Were education competence to increase, America's poverty rolls, which averaged about 13 percent over the last sixty years, could drop to 6.5 percent if not lower within a generation. This is an obtainable objective. Savings in today's dollars for Welfare and Anti-poverty programs would be reduced, about $500 billion (2020 dollars), or 10 percent of our national budget. Harder to measure is the reduction of crime and imprisonment, but it is not unreasonable to believe that crime could drop by half in a generation.

Is there evidence for this theory, a sniff test that tells us about results of more and better education? The infographic above may be a bit hard to read, but the statistics show that with improvement in education, many critical variables improve. The essential outcomes are these: the higher one's education level the 1) higher the worker's income, 2) the higher the likelihood of marriage, an essential anti-poverty institution, 3) and less likely the citizen will be imprisoned.

Specifically, the average weekly income of a high-school dropout is $606 a week compared to $864 for some college and $1281 for workers with a college degree. Even if every child graduates from high school with proficiency in all subjects, would every student progress toward a college education? Not likely, but the value of their education shows up in how well they qualify for any job they choose to seek. More important, a larger and larger cohort of students will seek some form of higher education including but not limited to a college education which will improve access to the evolving market for high-technology job and higher incomes.

Second, a success sequence—getting a quality education, a good job, marrying and then having children—has, over centuries—proven to assure economic health. According to the Bureau of Labor Statistics, three major labor market problems can hinder a worker's ability to earn an income that is above the poverty threshold: low earnings, periods of unemployment, and involuntary part-time employment. In 2018, 10.9 percent of families with only one member in the labor force for more than half the year were living below the poverty level. *"This compared with 1.3 percent for families with two or more members in the labor force,"* according to the Bureau of Labor Statistics.

The latter sentence is a measure of the Success Sequence. Depriving so many students of a quality education is creating an *education emergency* that will imperil our economic success and stifle vast swaths of workers' ability to pursue happiness. Assuring that our children get a quality education is the primary building block that allows workers to ascend the ladder of success, build families and improve their happiness. Had our education system provided a great education to all over the last sixty years, there is a good chance the poverty rate could be near the 1.3 percent. This rate should be our goal and measure of success.

With improved education for all, and had education been the root of America's anti-poverty efforts during this century, the reduction of social welfare costs, expenditures for imprisonment and property losses due to crime, would be reduced by an estimate $700 billion.

Solutions

Three possible solutions will help reset our path to education proficiency for all students. Each alternative aims to transfer the right to an education to the parent and child from state ownership.

The most straight forward approach is Education Enterprise Zones. EEZ permits groups of parents to ally and solicit bids from high-performing education institutions to propose options. These organizations should include any type of education provider including charter, public, private, online, religious, etc. EEZs could be established by state or federal governments, or with the collaboration of both. For states that do not wish to participate, parent funding could be backstopped by federal funds. Competing providers would be certified by the state or federal government and have a track record of very high proficiency performance, or an education plan that simulates a very successful provider.

A second path to education excellence is via a constitutional amendment. This is a much bigger challenge as it would require three-quarters of the states to ratify. As many states have strong public sector unions, reaching the goal of thirty-eight signatory states is unlikely. The mission of an amendment would be to take away a right to an education from the state and give it to parents and students. "Congress shall make no law prohibits the free access of parents and students to the education provider of their choice." The devil is in the details as poor parents should have access to charter like funding for their options and rich parents should be means-tested for funding. To achieve better education results, parents must be afforded more choices which they can test for value monthly and alter their education trajectory when performance lacks. A two-way street exists. The parents have contractual requirements as well. They need to become Chief Education Officers at home. Many charters mandate specific responsibilities for parents as a requirement for student registration. For education to be successful, both teach-side and learn-side components need collaboration and engagement.

Third, parents might consider unionizing to diminish the effects of public unions which are at odds with personal, national, and corporate education goals. This approach may produce a valuable dynamic whether either of the first two education solutions pass muster. The negative impact of unions closing schools during the COVID pandemic, regardless of scientific evidence provided by the CDC that schools should have been open, had a significant impact on parents. If parents organized politically, the power and negative impact of unions on our children's education could be diminished significantly.

To better understand how politics and unions play havoc with our children's education, a former union leader articulated the challenge. In 1985, the American Federation of Teachers President Albert Shanker was quoted as saying, "when school children start paying union dues, that's when I'll start representing the interests of school children." The lack of focus on our children's education showed up during COVID when unions made safety demands outside scientific evidence regarding the safety of our children and teachers in the classroom keeping schools closed to the detriment of our children. As unions focus and rules focused on teachers and administration, support for parents and students has waned. Rising responsibilities for school districts have increased staff counts and complexity of the delivery of an education without increasing performance. Increases in budgets should necessarily produce increases in performance. The union marketing shill is that we must spend more to get a better education. We have doubled our spending in real dollars over the last forty years with improving proficiency of our students. More pay is great and should be a goal, but better performance is essential for a successful America.

So, although parents' unions could be a helpful solution, our education crisis will not be averted by again doing the same thing which has been the modus operandi for decades. A constitutional amendment would be a very tough, long, partisan road and with a remarkably high barrier of ratification by thirty-eight states which would create a competitive market for parents to choose their best options. Though there in no easy path for Congress to pass legislation, Education Enterprise Zones—which are not unlike the Economic Enterprise Zones recently was passed by Congress—provide the most likely path to success.

Education inequality is the essential government challenge to a great economy, society and culture, and without education equality, a large swath of society has no ability to pursue happiness and no access to the first rung of economic success.

Transforming Retirement: Introducing the 501k

Our retirement system, like every public pension system in the world, is financially unsustainable and has been since its inception. Three major flaws in the initial design by FDR's brain trust assured financial malfunction. First, instead of floating the retirement age with life expectancy, which had been increasing rapidly during the first four decades of the century, the retirement age was fixed at sixty-five years of age. Second, the intergenerational tax, that workers would pay for retiree benefits, presumed that the ratio of workers to retirees would remain relatively constant. Since its inception, the ratio has declined from over 150:1 to 2.3:1 workers to retirees today. Finally, Social Security and Medicare originally targeted the poor, but over the decades Congress continually expanded the beneficiary pool to all Americans including people like Bill Gates, that is including rich citizens that do not need a check from the government.

The math sniff test for this intergenerational tax may have seemed reasonable at 1 percent of the first $3,000 of income in 1940. A surplus of dollars took care of the poor quite easily. But with the expansion of benefits and beneficiaries, by the 1980s, the above three demographics created financial fire alarms. Sirens sounded regarding the future bankruptcy of Medicare and Social Security beginning in the late 1990s, but nothing was done.

Though a savings-based system would have created the best financial benefit for Social Security's initial launch, this approach was impossible in 1936 because of technology shortcomings—there was no technology! Banking transactions were done by hand. Putting dollars from paychecks into passbook savings accounts was impossible! The technology problem is now a technology opportunity. Savings and investment transaction that employed high commissions last century are zero today, smoothing a transition for an intergenerational tax to a savings/investment solution vastly easier and smarter. The financial benefit is stunning. Whereas one dollar taxed for retirement is returned to beneficiaries as 98 cents, dollar saved/invested by a worker today with a 4.5 percent annual is worth $174 dollars upon retirement, perhaps more. The question is how to get from a system with failing financials based on never ending tax increases, to a savings-based solution.

Proposals for fixing the underfunding of our retirement system have cropped up over the last two decades. Solutions have included: ignore the problem and borrow the money ($50 trillion or more); tax the rich (they don't have enough money to fix the problem); reduce benefits by a third; a not well flushed out savings carveout for young workers proposed by Bust; or a continuation of tax increase. The Social Security Trust Fund Annual Report recommended increasing Medicare and Social Security taxes to 15.1 percent from 7.65 percent to erase the nearly $50 trillion in unfunded mandates. The $50 trillion deficit assumes an increase in life expectancy of eleven years this century (SSA estimate.) The likelihood that life-expectancy will only rise eleven years this century is extremely low. Were life expectancy rise to thirty-three additional years by the end of the century, as recommended by Longevity Institute Director Sr. David Sinclair, retirement taxes would zoom from 15.1 percent (employee plus employer taxes) to nearly 45 percent. As raising retirement taxes to 15.1 percent would likely crash the economy, imagine what 45 percent would do. Yet finding a remedy for the underfinancing of our retirement system has not been a priority for over 30 years.

If the reader has no memory of these options being proposed by Congresses or presidents, it is because these solutions do not make for good campaign rhetoric. Taxes have not fixed the funding problem, and more taxes will do great harm to our economy.

To keep the system afloat for the last eighty years, though, the tool of choice has been raising taxes. Since the program's inception, retirement taxes have been raised thirty-two times. Social Security tax rates are up 765 percent, and Medicare taxes are up 414 percent. Congress needs a solution, as does America and our children, but with the lack of evidence-based critical thinking and a dearth of innovative solution building, are leaders are AWOL.

The following proposal is a way forward financial sustainability of our retirement systems.

CIVIL Governance proposes transforming the retirement system with the 501K, a complement to the 401K, but available to all workers.

The CIVIL's 501K rests on three pillars:

First, add two years to the retirement age as quickly as possible to account for the two-year increase in life expectancy that already occurred this century;

then allow the retirement age to float up with life expectancy, replacing a static retirement age with a retirement age indexed to life expectancy. The equation for indexing retirement age would be written as current life expectancy (78.5) minus nine years or around 69.5 years. As life expectancy floats up, so too does the retirement age. Had FDR's brain trust done this is 1936, the system would be financially sustainable with retirement taxes of around 2 percent instead of today's 7.65 percent and there would be no future financing problem.

Second, update Medicare to a fixed benefit solution. To execute the final pillars, a fixed Medicare benefit produces the framework for means-testing retirement benefits.

Employing means-testing, today's top five percent of retirees, the richest of the rich, would need little or no dollars from the safety net as they have considerable wealth upon which to retire. The reasonable politician may be more inclined to accommodate fixed benefits for Medicare (a notion proposed in the past and rejected) because providing benefits to the rich was never necessary. The top 5 percent of earners consume about 12 percent of the benefits from the retirement system. An elderly billionaire recently suggested that the government send him a $3,000 check for social security each month that he does not need. The government should not be in the business of making the rich richer.

Altering the intergenerational tradeoff between workers and retirees from an expensive high tax for workers and universal benefits for the elderly, changes with means-testing. The budget reductions produced by increasing the retirement age 2.5 years, retirement-age indexing with life-expectancy and means-testing are significant. These changes will reduce the outlays from retirement programs that will allow a reduction of worker payroll taxes to be saved. Over time, the more Americans save translates into increasing financial sustainability; as fewer people need less help from government, this improves the finances for Social Security and Medicare trust funds. Over forty years, nest eggs in 501Ks will grow to around $100 trillion in forty years which gives a big lift to economic growth as well. Instead of a few percent of workers retiring as millionaires, over the long term as much as fifty percent of the population will retire rich.

Budget reductions from these three changes (indexing, means-testing and a 2.5-year retirement age increase) with some variance on how each is implemented, will range from 36 percent to 43 percent. These estimated budget savings will allow the individual tax rate to drop to 3.15 percent (from 7.65 percent) with 4.5 percent moved to personal 510K accounts. The business tax of 7.65 percent will remain for about twenty years, but as the retirement system becomes more financial sustainable, the business tax will gradually be reduced.

What are the program requirements?

- There is 501K guaranteed return on investments from private financial institutions. Only qualified institutions will participate and establish accounts not unlike the 401K. Individuals will choose from a menu of financial tools from private and public bonds, mutual funds and special Retirement Bonds. The guaranteed rate of return over rolling seven-years periods and must exceed 4.5 percent. Institutions that fail to meet this target will be removed from the list providers. Any shortfalls from failed institutions will be covered by the government.

What are the benefits?

- The CIVIL 501K will produce the biggest tax cut in history for the poor and middle class. Most important, the nest eggs of the poorest—consider the minimum wage worker for the last fifty years—would have *$100,000 in the 501K*. This is more savings than two-thirds of workers retiring today.

- National wealth (the total of personal nest eggs) will grow to $100 trillion dollars over the next forty years. At a minimum, increasing wealth and decreasing retirement program costs will improve economic growth another 1 percent to 2 percent. The increased investment base will also increase employment.

- Overall cost reductions in the system will vastly reduce retirement underfunding if not erase it.

- The cost of retirement programs will decline over time, reducing deficit pressures. Over the first forty years, half of retirees will need no help from the safety net, reducing the cost of the safety net by more than 70 percent. Under the most optimistic of metrics, this number could rise to 90 percent.

- The initial savings rate would be 4.65 percent of the current 7.65 percent retirement taxes, reducing the tax portion to 3 percent. With more wealth created for workers each year, after twenty years, savings rates will grow to 6 percent (of the current 7.65 percent tax) and a 1.65 percent tax for the safety net. The employer tax contribution would begin to fall from 7.65 percent at year 20 and by year 40 should be around 1.65 percent

- Net-net: Fewer and lower taxes, a highly served safety net for the poor, gains in wealth for all, and an economy with increased growth between 1 percent and 2 percent annually, doubling the average GDP average this century of a little more than 2 percent.

That politicians over the last eighty years expanded the footprint of the beneficiary population from the poor to everyone, the continued requirement for increasing taxes should have rung a cautionary financial bell with Congress. The political sniff test, that everyone was covered, certainly had political merit. Rising life expectancy occurred in front of our eyes and our increasing scientific understanding of the human genome should have set off financial warnings that called for innovation and transformation, but politics intruded. Social Security and Medicare became a third rail. "Touch it and you die." Why? Because instead of working together to seek a remedy, each political party used any potential remedy as campaign invective against opponents.

Conclusion: Evidence-Based Planning

Retirement and Education are only two examples of America's twenty-first century challenges. How to construct new solutions based on the available data, though, is central to better governance. Transiting from political decision making is essential for good decision-making and great planning. Because politics thinks in short snippets, it is regressive and harmful.

Evidentiary planning has enormous financial benefits. Transforming just two of America's failing institutions, retirement and education, America's finances would vastly improve. As noted earlier, were these two changes implemented ten years ago, the 2020 budget (outside of the spending for COVID initiatives) would have been $3.2 trillion instead of $4.8 trillion. The savings accrued: about $800 billion in reduced expenses paid to rich retirees who means-tested out of part or all of benefits due to the increased wealth.

Increased education proficiency leads to higher pay; increased family formation would add another $500 billion (possibly as high as $800 billion) in savings. Initiatives for simplicity, innovation and quality results in government and in regulation would return as much as $1 trillion in compliance costs back to the economy, and another $300 billion in unnecessary or non-productive spending by the government.

Until great results from our government determine political will, and not big money donors, evidence-based government will suffer.

Even with only a smattering of the scientific method introduced to political activities, America can be a better place. This is the mission of CIVIL Governance. Its broader ten-point strategic plan follows at the end of this book.

CHINA VERSUS AMERICA

WHEN DENG XIAOPING REPLACED MAO Zedong upon his death, the west was encouraged by the economic and social reforms adopted by China. The Chinese transformation aligned with our hopes for a friendly economic competition that would encourage both economic and political liberalization. Deng's strategy, though, was to, "Hide your capacities and bide your time." Put another way, the strategy was to get their economy running well enough to quietly take their appropriate leadership position at the top of the international heap. Most western nations assumed that as the Chinese economy improved so too would the social and political restrictions of the Communist Party. The opposite has occurred. President Xi used his newly minted Capitalist dollars to enrich the rich of the totalitarian state.

Rather than hope for the best and plan for the worst, American and western nations' motto is instead: *Hope is our strategy.* Maybe if we look the other way, things will turn out fine. Probably not.

In 2013, as Xi Jinping took the helm of the Chinese Communist Party, with a deep Communist resume, he took a sharp turn toward a more aggressive China. In two short years, the Politburo published a comprehensive, thirty-year, economic, political, and military strategy to assume international leadership. Gone was the Hide and Bide strategy of Deng, and yet the West clung to old hopes that China would remain a friendly rival. By 2018, eyes were opening in Washington. The Chinese had not only built islands in the South China Sea to expand their territorial rights, but they claimed international sea and border rights around the islands with numerous incursions on the open seas which were meant to enforce their claims. Since 2018, approximately 2 million Uyghurs have been imprisoned for reeducation. China has clashed in 2019-20 in eastern Ladakh with India over border alignment. By 2020, when China guillotined political and civil rights in Hong Kong, a much harder totalitarian line was drawn, but it is still unclear that our government, as well as other Western nations, have fully embraced China as an aggressive opponent versus a friendly competitor. Though America's changing view regarding Chinese trade and investment is apparent, America still has no strategy to increase economic output or reign in Chinese growth. Status quo reigns at our own peril.

Our competition with China has the feel of Lute Olsen planning for them, and Ben Lindsay planning for us.

China's calculus silently in tow for decades is a simple one. As Deng recommended increasing the pool of pathbreakers with new ideas, he understood China had the premier position because the population topped 1.4 billion compared to the US's 225 million (circa 1980.) They could produce five times the number of ideas, thus five times the amount of potential economic activity. Conversely, there needed to be only one-fifth as intense exploiting of Capitalism to achieve the economic goals. To succeed, they did not need to work as hard to reap the benefits of Capitalism. China did not have to work as hard at Capitalism to beat us at our own game. They believed they could retain their Communist dictatorship with just a splash of Capitalism, and that strategy is working. As President Xi China's aggressive intent increases along with their GDP, the west needs a unified plan to keep Chinese economic and military threats at bay, diminishing China's ambitions by cutting down their economic access to world markets. President Trump turned the lights on to China's ambitions. Biden's direction as of April 2021 is not fully clear, but he appears to align with Trump's approach.

The state of the competition today? While America bickers over divergent policy differences between the political parties, the operations of our government are so terribly mismanaged that we have unfunded mandates (spending without revenue) of $200 trillion (the low estimate) over the next seventy-five years. Our social programs either are not financially sustainable or are not fulfilling their social objectives or both. The mismanagement by both parties translates into an average 2 percent growth this century with no plan fixing our operational shortcoming so that America could grow more quickly.

China on the other hand will likely grow at 6 percent a year during this decade and perhaps at this rate for the foreseeable future. This translates into a win for China. At these growth rates, China will assume the number one economy before 2030, and likely be twice the size of America's economy by 2050. Because of their vast wealth, instead western civilization and the rule of law as the foundation of the international community, Communists will call the shots and the west will be kicked to the curb.

For America to compete and win the Chinese competition, and for that matter for the rest of the modern world to compete and win against the new Communistic paradigm, new thinking about governance is required. That Socialism, nor the more piecemeal Socialist approach, does not work well, but is, on occasion required, updating our economic model for building, and optimizing social monopolies is essential. Simple, evidence-based, results-graded monopolies are required for a best run government. Constant attention to results and updates and transformations when results go awry will assure the evolution of programs toward better and better value for all Americans. For the rest of the economy, plan for the competition is essential, using the same evidenced-based formulation.

Western law and tradition have built a magnificent infrastructure for success. The question is: What new tools are needed to compete with this new alternative to Marxian Communism and how will a better set of leaders focus on quality of governance, not the quantity of spending. Without clear-eyed focus on best-run government, our children may live under the heavy hand of spreading dictatorships around the world, all behind a single, powerful dictatorship in Beijing.

Who Wins the Economic Sweepstakes

Today's competition is a new, century-long, cold war. The winner will be the government that can find a winning formula for success. China's slide back to a strong central government with a heavy hand on its people will begin to strangle ideas that are crucial to future economic growth. America's slide to a stronger and stronger central government will have the same debilitating effect on the economy, producing more poorly run government programs, bigger government and more dollars in the government's hands instead of the hands of the citizens. It's as if both competitors are trying to lose the competition. If these trajectories are accurate, though, China will win the competition, if only because of its 1.4 billion population.

Have faith, though. The trend over the last ten thousand years has been, as Adam Smith suggested, toward improvement. Failure generally leads to success. America is much like Edison's light bulb; it took a thousand tries to get it right, and thousands more after he perfected it so that today I am provided an affordable LED bulb. Our freedom to change, to update, to transform after we have failed will be the ultimate elixir of success. With great hope, the political swing to the Left, toward a more autocratic, centrally planned economic and society, will diminish as an option for the voter, resulting in government by common sense.

FINAL THOUGHTS

BECAUSE SO MANY AMERICANS DISTRUST government, it is not a stretch to believe that part of our angst from a sinking feeling is that our federal government is so poorly run that it is leaderless and rudderless. In fact, most government organizations across the country are very poorly run, and the federal government, because of its enormity, is the worst run organization in our nation and the world. Were the federal government a publicly traded stock on the DOW, its price would be negative. Politics and partisanship have trumped common sense, wisdom and critical thinking. Our government and its poor stewardship should make us blush.

The path out of this growing nightmare is not easy if only because poor judgment and power-peddling leadership is such a well-ingrained habit that poorly conceived spending on poorly conceived programs and policy have become a daily political fix for politicians and political junkies. "Look at how much money we spent," is the happy refrain from politicians hoping to be re-elected. Even more challenging, big contributions by business, unions and special interests solidify worst practices and status quo solutions that did not work well last century. Political parties, the media, and the citizenry have become two gigantic echo chambers where members of each silo take verbal potshots across the DMZ. The Internet echo chamber contains dutiful partisans, retweeting angry language to the delight of each faction. This is great for profits and political contributions, but it only increases the partisanship and political divergence.

Big money is the central problem for promulgating the status quo and power politics. Only the voter can change this ride to nowhere by giving only to candidates that take the CIVIL $195 pledge, no big money, period. The small-money approach deprives big donors of power as well as the political parties' ability to leverage big money for non-stop advertising which voters have come to hate. Of course, if the 90 percent of eligible voters who do not give, gave only $10 a month for a few months, small donations would vastly outpace big donors, changing the political landscape for good. That would be the key to a better run America. If power politics begins to lose its voting and lobbyists are seen for what they really are, purveyors of the status quo, then the no-big-money candidates and their voters become the future for America politics.

The big money also solidifies the divergence of governing principles, one set predominately driven by bigger and bigger government, a Socialist approach (the Dems), and bigger and bigger government via a not so limited federal government (Reps). Though politicians of either ilk spend vastly, without good results, how they approach government is so vastly different that each election means that whatever was done the previous two years will be undone by a new legislative majority and/or a new president. Basically, we are going nowhere, slowly.

Hope for the best, plan for the worst.

My request to the reader: First, realize that reading a single news source assures that only half the story is conveyed. The media has become so partisan that news and editorials rehash information from one political party's point of view or the other. A news article prints the truth, but only enough to support the narrative of one party or the other. This novel approach to news spawned 'fake news,' but the news is not so much fake or false, as it leaves out important facts that would give the news balance.

Scott Adams, creator of *Dilbert*, wrote in the *Wall Street Journal* that if you read something from a news source from one side of the political spectrum and then you read a source from the other side, and they agree, then the information was probably true. If they didn't agree, then wait a couple of weeks and see what happens. Americans are stuck in the political volatility because the press is the willing instigator of our separation. As ninety percent of the press, media and Internet are slanted Democrat, it is amazing the Republicans win any election. On the upside, perhaps most of us cut through the media fog or ignore it. On the downside, having no single source of the unjaded truth has created vast pools of distrust and anger in the populace.

Second, seek out Independent candidates that have a better proposition for governing, persons that are neither D nor R, but something new and inventive.

Third, join the CIVIL movement and be a voter that has new ideas that could help propel our platforms into the exceptional hands of millions of Americans who are looking for a better future.

Hope for the best but have a plan. The constant evolution of ideas in a free society works slowly but surely. Washington has become the ultimate killer of new ideas as they recycle old ideas and guarantee that old, failing programs and policy never die. Freedoms—especially our freedom to create new ideas—should not be eroded during our political cataclysm. Hope, but plan for the worst. Quit giving money to these political parties. Find nonpartisans to vote for, people that have a better vision for the future—and a plan to compete and defeat China's economic onslaught. Our children need you.

– Tom

CIVIL: A STRATEGIC PLAN

WILL OUR TWO TRADITIONAL PARTIES find common ground on their own? It's highly unlikely, so a disruption of the political process is important. America needs new ideas and a political referee in Washington that can bring the warring parties to the table.

The over-riding challenge of Federalism 2.0, Federalism with evidence-based policy formulation, a CIVIL Strategy, is the political war between the Democrats and Republicans. It is all consuming, nonstop, and angry. There is no room for political transformation because every moment and every dollar spent is traded for political power to extend the status quo of both political parties. There is no voice in the center. In fact, there is no center, no collaboration, no path forward, only anger and animus. The center is a vast wasteland.

Is there a need for a new political movement? Absolutely. Without one, it is hard to imagine that the two political parties can rise above the hate, anger, and irreconcilable differences to collaborate on America's most significant problems. We are talking *past* one another at the water cooler just as we are talking *by* one another over the legislative divide. We have two parties, two political cultures, and there is no longer anyone representing the middle. CIVIL is committed to engaging the American voter and the two political parties to transform retirement programs, assure that educational opportunity is available to parents whose children are enrolled in failing subpar schools, and to reform our anti-poverty programs so that we reduce the number of citizens in poverty. The CIVIL Strategic Plan is a new path that is a continuation of America's constant evolution toward better governance. America is in a very rough spot as we have been so many times since our founding, but there is a path to vastly better government and politics. The CIVIL Platform encompasses ten strategies and programs. Like any new ideas, they need to be tested. They need to evolve and improve. As any new ideas are vetted, these are the starting points in the race to American success in the twenty-first century.

The crucial element of creating a new movement is to fill the vacuum in the center. Democrats and Republicans have no common ground to engage a conversation about fixing America's biggest problems because the Left wants big, strong, expensive government and Conservatives bend toward federalism's limited government approach: Democratic Socialism versus Democratic Capitalism. When one party proposes a new policy, the Twitter guns rise from the other foxhole and start shooting. Anger rises, tempers flare. Donation letters are sent. If anything is agreed upon, it is only that we are going to spend more—on everything. The art of collaboration is gone.

Americans do the same at home. Many a Thanksgiving dinner was cut short by inflamed language. Political talk at the water cooler has been diminished for fear of infuriating our office mates because one or the other does not follow a particular party line of thought.

This case for at least one new party, if not more, is important so that the bipolar world has a third option to triangulate. This is the case for CIVIL, the movement in the middle, bringing new ideas and a new vision to a third wheel with a different path forward, to be the referee, to mitigate the anger when the Twitter pistols are drawn. Without a new political movement, this country will continue to stew in its own anger, setting us up for a dystopian future run by China.

Evidence-Based Government: Ten CIVIL Transformations

The following transformations are the CIVIL Platform. They provide a path forward to self-regulate campaign spending to small donations; a path to less expensive campaigns; and they lay out a series of economic and social makeovers that will increase economic growth to around 4.5 percent per year. At this growth rate, American economic leadership over China will be retained at least past mid-century.

The following ten transformations are a 2020 update to the five proposals in the Great Experiment II. As noted previously, had these ten solutions been in place since 2010, not only would our economy have grown much faster—4.5 percent—but the streamlining of government would have reduced outlays by $1.6 trillion dollars in 2020, decreasing our budget from $4.8 trillion to $3.2 trillion.

#1 CIVIL, A New Strategy and Movement

For over one hundred years, Democrats and Republicans have been writing election laws which erect high barriers to entry for new political parties, preventing competitive access to their duopoly. Over the last 120 years over forty new parties have tried to accommodate the challenges of legal barriers created by nominating petitions and voting thresholds—and none have consistently succeeded in placing federal candidates.

The most recent competitors, the Libertarians and Greens, have a hard time staying on state ballots. In Arizona, it appears the Greens will fall off the ballot unless they acquire (again) another 30,000 plus petition signatures this election cycle.

The two-party system is great. The problem isn't the system. It's our two, angry, power-hungry, political parties—if you are worried about greed in business. Political greed is proportional to the amount of money spent by our government, which is $4.8 trillion (2020), twenty times the size of an average Fortune 500 business. The parties are fully focused on retaining their power and placing partisanship over the needs of our nation. This places our nation at risk. Partisan sniping and yelling even hampered the debate of the Coronavirus bill on the floor of the Senate. It is disheartening to watch the desire for political power replace the quality leadership focused on citizens most in need. The problem isn't the two-party system; it's our political parties.

In *Why America Is Stuck With Only Two Parties*, Micah Sifry states: "Republican and Democrat-controlled legislatures swiftly learned that they could use this power (legal barriers to entry) to smother rising third parties like the Populist Party and gave themselves automatic lines on the ballot while instituting onerous petitioning requirements to hinder other upstarts."

New parties, hoping to enter the political marketplace, must spend hundreds of thousands of dollars to get nominating petitions signed, and, once on the ballot, if they miss the required vote tally threshold, they must start over with nominating petitions to get the party back on the ballot for the next election cycle.

This is purposely and prohibitively expensive and meant to kill competition from new parties.

Arizona requires 31,686 signatures (and another 1,783 for the candidate) for a new party and candidate to attain ballot status with the potential cost above $200,000. To attain ballot status in all states would likely cost over $10 million. It's a big hill to climb. Like any monopoly Democrats and Republicans are protecting their turf at all costs. What is the best option to assure the voter has more choices in the general election? CIVIL proposes endorsing Independent candidates who adopt the CIVIL platform. No new party is required, but competition is assured. CIVIL will also endorse candidates from any political party that endorses our platform.

Beyond petition requirement, most states also employ a presidential or gubernatorial vote threshold for new parties to stay on the ballot. The threshold varies by state from 2 percent to 5 percent of the total vote tallies. Missing any barrier means the party must start the petitioning process over again for the next election cycle, at great expense.

The Serve America Movement (SAM) is a great example of a new party challenging the status quo. They gained ballot access in New York in 2018 and ran a candidate for governor. During the 2020 election cycle, the state legislature is considering adding another barrier for new party entry: A party must also obtain at least 130,000 votes for governor or president in the general election to retain ballot access. The enormous expense of gaining and retaining ballot access protects powerful monopolies whose ideas are stuck in concrete having been laid in previous centuries.

In *Breaking the Two-Party Doom Loop,* Lee Drutman writes "Toxic politics destroys trust in institutions and in fellow citizens. Unremedied. It kills Democracy." Drutman recommends having more political parties as the solution for diminishing the anger between the two parties. CIVIL agrees. Without new political parties, the toxicity will only increase. The CIVIL approach is much the same. Without a non-partisan referee, the two major political parties will continue to rail to a single end: more political power, and more and more big money to fund their power. The voter needs more and better choices.

Regarding governing principles, CIVIL's platform is neither Leftist nor Conservative. It is a political movement covering the middle ground. Its aim is to provide simpler, more efficient, results-oriented government that runs smart with less expense and without anger and animus. CIVIL's objective is to be the referee, bringing transformative ideas upon which both parties can agree.

The voters deserve better policy, more civil politics, smarter government, and far fewer barriers to new ideas to compete with the current, backward-looking parties who are more concerned about their power and their money than the needs of the people.

#2 Take the CIVIL $195 Pledge

Limit Campaign Donations Without New Laws:

Americans should ask every candidate to take the CIVIL $195 Pledge. The challenge simply asks each candidate to take no donations over $195 and to agree to forgo all large campaign donations and to promote civility in elections and government operations.

Sixty-one percent of voters believe neither party represents them and 51 percent are looking for a new party.

If employees in a business felt this way about their company, it would be out of business. The same is true for your church, a nonprofit, for any institution. Without trust, without feeling you have a voice, institutions die.

What drives the bad behavior, the yelling and screaming and the Twitter wars in Washington? Big money has created two insulated, angry, and power-hungry political parties. The individuals in the parties are good people. The institutions, so focused on accumulating and keeping their immense power, have become corrupted and very protective of the monied interests, their source of power. They are like two giant dinosaurs, loaded down with money bags and dragging us to the tar pits.

How big are the donations? According to Open Secrets, the top one hundred givers to federal campaigns gave $790 million in 2018, about 23 percent of all donations. *Just one hundred people!* Seventy percent of all donations are from large donors, about ½ of one percent of eligible voters. Another $3.2 billion is spent by lobbyists whose sponsors are big business, big unions, and big special interests to influence and write our laws. These donors are not giving out of the goodness of their hearts. They are buying power and influence.

The rich are buying power and influence and writing laws for their benefit, and the common guys like you and I cannot buy a vowel. The rich do not need our help at being rich!

As there is zero likelihood of passing legislation to reduce sizable donations, the need for better options is now. The political parties need to regulate themselves, and so do the candidates.

The vision of CIVIL is to lead by example, challenge the status-quo and incite change by doing. We look forward to hearing from each candidate with their support for our CIVIL initiative for this election and all upcoming elections, in 2020 and beyond.

Take the Pledge!

While voting, instead of voting Democrat or Republican, find an Independent candidate that is endorsed by CIVIL. You will be glad you did.

#3 Financially Sustainable Retirement System

Transforming Federal Retirement Programs with Lower Taxes?
An Economic Bump to Restart the Economy

Proposals for fixing the underfunding of our retirement system have cropped up over the last two decades. Solutions have included: ignore the problem and borrow the money; tax the rich; reduce benefits by a third; or increase taxes. The Social Security Trust Fund Annual Report recommended increasing Medicare and Social Security taxes to 15.1 percent from 7.65 percent to erase the nearly $50 trillion in unfunded mandates.

If the reader has no memory of these options being proposed by Congresses or presidents, it is because these solutions do not make for good campaign rhetoric; they do not fix the funding problem, and they would do great harm to our economy.

Are there other options? Not in Washington.

Getting outside the Beltway echo chambers is necessary. Thinking like a political entrepreneur, like an outsider—a political unicorn—is essential.

What lies at the core of the underfunding? First, while the Social Security retirement age has increased by only two years since the program's inception,

Americans are living an average of seventeen years longer. Second, the retirement system, which was focused originally on the poor, now provides benefits to everyone, even the richest.

To keep the system afloat for the last eighty years, the tool of choice has been raising taxes. Since the program's inception, retirement taxes have been raised thirty-two times; Social Security tax rates are up 765 percent, and Medicare taxes are up 414 percent. Increasing taxes to the Social Security Administration's (SSA) proposed 15.1 percent would be the largest increase for poor and middle-class workers in history.

If increased taxes have not stayed the financial bloodletting, then what could produce a financially sustainable retirement system?

Enter the CIVIL 501K, a complement to the 401K, which is today available to only about half of our citizens.

The CIVIL's 501K rests on three pillars:

First, allow the retirement age to float up with life expectancy, replacing a static age. The late Harvard economist Martin Feldstein argued that the retirement age needs to increase. CIVIL recommends two and a half years. The equation for retirement age would be written as current life expectancy (78.5) minus nine years or around 69.5 years.

Second, update Medicare to a fixed benefit solution. Under the 501K plan, a fixed benefit would allow Congress to means-test the wealthiest, such as billionaires, so that they pay their fair share into the nation's retirement system.

Third, with means testing, today's top five percent of retirees would need little or no dollars from the safety net. The reasonable politician may be more inclined to accommodate fixed benefits because no one wants our kids to endure that 15.1 percent tax rate to pay for the $50 trillion in underfunding of the current system.

Each of these recommendations reduce the federal retirement budget between 10 and 15 percent. As these reductions increase over time, workers can add a larger and larger portion of their retirement taxes into their 501K.

What are the benefits?

- The CIVIL 501K will produce the biggest tax cut in history for the poor and middle class. Most important, the nest eggs of the poorest—consider the minimum wage worker for the last fifty years—would have *$100,000 in the 501K*. This is more savings than two-thirds of workers retiring today.

- National wealth (the total of personal nest eggs) will grow to $100 trillion dollars over the next forty years. At a minimum, increasing wealth and decreasing retirement program costs will improve economic growth another .50 percent to 1.0 percent.

- Overall cost reductions in the system will vastly reduce retirement underfunding if not erase it.

- The cost of retirement programs will decline over time, reducing deficit pressures. Over the first forty years, half of retirees will need no help from the safety net, reducing the cost of the safety by more than 70 percent. Under the most optimistic of metrics, this number could rise to 90 percent. Had the 501K been in place the last few decades, the current $1 trillion deficit would be close to zero.

- The initial savings rate would be 4.65 percent of the current 7.65 percent retirement taxes, reducing the tax portion to 3 percent. With more wealth created for workers each year, after twenty years, savings rates will grow to 6 percent (of the current 7.65 percent tax) and a 1.65 percent tax for the safety net. The employer tax contribution would begin to fall as well.

- Net-net: Fewer and lower taxes, a highly served safety-net for the poor, gains in wealth for all, and an economy with increased growth as high as an additional 1 percent.

#4 CIVIL's Education Enterprise Zones

A Parent's Right to a Quality Education Should Not Be Abridged

For three generations, parents in the inner city and rural America have been forced to enroll their children in public schools that are underperforming or failing. They should not have had to wait more than a *month*, much less five decades to access a high-quality education.

It is not for lack of effort or good intentions that local, state, and federal governments have not delivered; however, there is no reason that parents and students in underperforming schools shouldn't have the numerous options that rich parents have in the suburbs. *It's just not fair.* Over five decades, combative politics has built a two-class education system, one for the haves and one for the have-nots. This is education inequality at its worst and should not be tolerated. Education Enterprise Zones (EEZ) can help. Education Enterprise Zones will ensure that parents of students in failing schools have alternatives comparable to the numerous quality school choices available for wealthier parents' kids.

The purpose of Education Enterprise Zones is to put the right to a public education in the hands of parents, not politicians, bureaucrats, and unions.

Education Enterprise Zones will allow families stuck with failing or underperforming schools to self-organize and invite education providers to propose alternative schools. Enterprise Education Coupons will be provided to parents to enroll students in the new education solutions of their choice. School options may include charters, private, online, home schooling, and religious institutions.

The U.S. Department of Education will provide best practices culled from the best K-12 schools in America so that new education providers have a head start on good processes that have already succeeded across the United States. States may provide additional insights. Additionally, federal and state departments of education will deliver success benchmarks for each year so parents can measure the quality of their children's progress.

Like an economic enterprise zone, an education zone will provide regulatory relief and financing for their children's education that would otherwise be impossible in the current political climate. For parents in states that do not wish to participate financially, the federal government would provide funding. The aim is for registering parents to acquire at least three school solutions from which the parent group can choose to register their children. Schools could be broken into K-3, 4-6, 7-9 and high school with starting enrollment ranges beginning at 150 students.

Over the last fifty years, local, state, and federal government initiatives for improving education, especially for inner city and rural schools, included busing, budgetary equalization, Title IX, No Child Left Behind, Common Core, and a doubling, in real dollars, of education spending. Yet, outcomes have continued to decline. Without parent engagement and options that transform the culture of education for the student, all the money in the world will not achieve better results.

CIVIL believes that, as the ultimate purchaser of education, parents, as customers, have a right to choose the quality of education they want for their children, and if their first choice fails, they deserve alternative solutions. The problem with public schools is that they cannot fail and repeating their failures year after year has destroyed the education culture.

America's education report card has not been good. According to the National Assessment of Education Progress (NAEP), proficiency results show the challenge: 37 percent of twelfth graders are proficient in reading, 25 percent in math, and 22 percent in science. Economics, history and geography fared no better. *Results for inner-city schools are on average about ten points lower.* For an industrial economy in the 1930s, NAEP's test results would have been adequate. For a twenty-first century knowledge economy, these results need to be flipped so that 63 percent of students—or more!—are proficient in reading and 75 percent and 78 percent respectively for math and science.

Our education system needs an update and Education Enterprise Zones will allow competition that will increase education quality and outcomes. Bill Gates has recommended more education choice. EEZ provides much broader choices for the students most in need of a quality education.

If the U.S. economy is to accelerate into this century, to beat the mediocre 2.1 percent growth rate over the last twenty years, and to compete effectively against China's thirty-year plan to kick western civilization to the curb, our education system must ensure that every student is proficient in math, science, reading, and writing. We must prepare our children to compete for twenty-first century jobs or they will lose the competition to robots.

The costs of a poor education vastly increase the likelihood a child will drop out of school, have a more difficult time getting a good job, and decrease the likelihood of engaging in the most important economic success event of a lifetime, marriage. Our anti-poverty programs have not reduced poverty over the last fifty years because our schools are unable to educate those children most in need of climbing onto the first rung of economic success: an education. The number of people leaving poverty is equal to the number entering poverty due to the lack of an education.

Today, bright, talented kids in poor neighborhoods throughout our country are being sacrificed to prop up failed schools. Without a quality education, many will approach the job market without the necessary credentials for even a subsistence level job; many will lead limiting lives hampered by the social ills we are all too aware of; and others will wind up in prison. The cycle of inter-generational poverty and broken lives continues.

A diverse education market in our poorer communities will produce options for a good or great education giving children most in need a better shot at *their* Pursuit of Happiness.

#5 CIVIL's Success Factors Anti-Poverty Program

How the Pursuit of Happiness is Crucial to the New War on Poverty!

Since the advent of the War on Poverty in the late 1960s, the poverty rate has gone up or down, a couple of percentage points, generally related to the rise and fall of the economy. The underlying challenge: Because there are so many failing schools, the number of young adults flowing into the system closely aligns with those who have exited poverty.

Reducing poverty will occur only when public policy tightly entwines a quality education with job availability with encouragement for marriage and family, a linkage that produces economic success and an improved path to personal happiness.

Three factors form the foundation for personal economic success and happiness: 1) a high quality high school education and more when possible, 2) work and a willingness to improve one's job skills, and 3) marriage, family, and a stable home life.

To date, our programs presume that lack of money is the cause of poverty. Since the start of the War on Poverty in the 1960s, $40 trillion has been spent on a variety of anti-poverty programs, and these dollars have not diminished poverty. Though programs like SNAP, Medicare, Medicaid, and many others are an important safety net for those in need, they are not anti-poverty solutions because they do not reduce poverty.

To reduce poverty, we need to employ factors in success that have a proven track record.

An education, like money, will not buy happiness, but an education will increase the chances of acquiring a good job, which increases the opportunities for marriage and family, both of which increase economic success and confer a higher degree of happiness. If America is going to get serious about our Pursuit of Happiness, which requires reducing poverty, we must start with quality education.

To that end, CIVIL proposes Education Enterprise Zones to free parents and students from failing and underperforming schools. Over the last several generations, as employment has increasingly favored a strong mind over a strong back, education has become the cornerstone of a successful economic life. The more education one acquires, the more one's chances of acquiring a quality job increase, as does the likelihood of marriage and family. Additionally, marriage and family increase industriousness, which also produces higher degrees of happiness.

Ron Haskins of the Brookings Institute codified this approach in *The Success Sequence*. He states, "Our research shows that of American adults who followed these three simple rules, only about 2 percent are in poverty and nearly 75 percent have joined the middle class (defined as earning around $55,000 or more per year). There are surely influences other than these principles at play but following them guides a young adult away from poverty and toward the middle class."

America needs a safety net. There should be no doubt about that. But America also needs a simple, effective strategy that builds a success plan that starts in kindergarten and continues into early adulthood. A new anti-poverty system needs to focus on quality education, work, marriage, and family, in this order.

Five pillars build the CIVIL Success Factor approach:

- Anti-poverty solutions, beginning in kindergarten, require a new focus on education, especially in the inner city and rural America (Education Enterprise Zones).
- Work as a qualifying requirement for government assistance not only creates a foundation for personal success but is a key factor for increasing one's happiness.
- Equalize assistance to married and unmarried couples. The existing "welfare penalty" provides less assistance to married couples.
- Develop a personal success plan for each person in poverty.
- Limit the length of time that assistance is available.

This is a twenty-year project to reduce poverty rates by transforming the government's 'send-a-check" mentality, the traditional welfare state that makes poverty comfortable. Instead, we need policies that focus on personal success, with education as central to its anti-poverty strategy.

If we can raise the poor, those most in need, by absolutely assuring access to a quality education, we turn off the spigot of people entering poverty for lack of an education, the first rung of economic success.

According to most surveys of happiness around the world, work, marriage, and family are three of the most important elements to achieving a high degree of happiness. What has changed over the last fifty years is that much of America's anti-poverty efforts have not supported these factors. The CIVIL Success Factors approach is a starting point for reducing the poverty rate from 13 percent to 5 percent or less over the next twenty years.

#6 CIVIL: Congressional Chief Innovation and Simplicity Office

Simplicity Office Could Reduce the Cost of Government $480 Billion

Founding father Alexander Hamilton, one of America's most financially astute innovators, advised that "the true test of good government is its aptitude and tendency to produce a good administration." Good administration is not a description of our government's stewardship. Since our federal government is a $4.8 trillion enterprise, and the most complicated and expensive administrative entity in the world—often with no results to show—it is little wonder that 80 percent of Americans distrust it. America needs smarter, simpler, more innovative government to streamline this muddled organization and to compete with the rest of the world.

Our federal government is too big, too expensive, resultless and costly. Critical thinking went out along with any sensibility of how to spend our tax dollars effectively.

We need a new legislative and executive branch culture that provides guidance in erecting simpler, more manageable regulatory, financial, and administrative processes. Given the vast system of departments, agencies, and grant programs, little effort is made to assure that what government does erect has measurable objectives for success. Our tax dollars are spent in abundance, but are they spent well? Do dollars spent translate into positive paybacks, or are dollars merely spent and then totaled as though spending were the only intent that mattered?

CIVIL recommends the establishment of a Chief Innovation and Simplicity Office.

Over the last ten centuries, from Occam to Einstein, science has accepted the notion that the simplest solution is most likely the best solution. Einstein noted that, "If you can't explain it to a six-year-old, you don't understand it yourself." Complexity defines the tax code, the Obamacare legislative and regulatory framework, and just about any legislation. Complexity is easy. Just keep adding and adding and adding. In government, scopes expand and expand and expand. In business, new items are adding to workflows and business processes. In our personal lives, we do not have time for complexity. We prefer to, "Keep it simple, stupid."

All institutions fall prey to complexity. A former CEO of a major enterprise software company warned that complexity costs up to ten percent of profits. Imagine our federal government, which is nearly 200 times the size of the average Fortune 500 company, losing track of 10 percent of the federal budget. Thomas Jefferson warned future generations: "The natural progress of things is for the government to gain ground and for liberty to yield."

The Federal Government is a monied leviathan that will spend $4.8 trillion this year and publishes between 70,000 and 80,000 pages of rules and regulations a year. As the leviathan has grown, our trust in government has plummeted to less than 20 percent. But if both parties can continue to use government spending and regulation to buy votes and power, there is no reason to change the current culture. HERE

The mission of a Chief Simplicity & Innovation Officer (CSIO) would be fourfold and combining mission and CSIO responsibilities to do the following:

- Propose a simplicity process for drafting any proposals or programs. Numerous processes are available, but the House needs to collaborate on acceptable rules and processes.

- Review the House and Senate rules and make recommendations to voters and the government for changes that would simplify legislative and regulatory processes, and mandate measurable objectives for legislation so that their outcomes can be scored.

- Institute an X-Prize to be used either at the direction of Congress or the president, or by the CSIO as a tool to seek alternative solutions to be considered by the Congress/president. The CSIO will review each regulation in the Federal Register, and for each needed regulation, run an X-Prize to find the simplest, least expensive solution.

- Review every spending program and grant to evaluate whether it should be continued or terminated; measure the success of the solution or legislation with respect to the original stated goals of the initiative or law.

The X-Prize will be a great political lever to publish winning ideas, giving the voter leverage to promote best in class solutions and for legislators to reduce their dependence on lobbyists and special interests.

What might a simpler solution look like for major legislation passed over the last decade?

When the Trump Administration proposed tax cuts in 2017, the objectives were to reduce taxes and simplify the tax code. What happened? Congress raised the standard deduction, which reduced the number of tax filers who can itemize deductions; the tax code grew in length and complexity; and the rich reaped the greatest benefit from deductions and credits.

A more innovative approach would be to toss out the tax code and tax income at the effective tax rate, i.e., the percentage of taxes paid after deductions. The tax form would be a post card, or no card at all, and the revenues would be the same. As an example, I am in the 22 percent tax bracket, but with deductions, my effective tax rate is only 14 percent. Those deductions are out of reach for the typical taxpayer. The biggest obstacles to tax simplification are lobbyists whose wealthy, powerful clients benefit from complexity.

The Affordable Care Act (ACA) suffers the same complexity problem. The original intent of the ACA was to ensure that citizens with pre-existing conditions could purchase insurance. Less than 1 million people were affected. Twenty thousand pages long, the ACA's architecture was constructed with 153 committees to manage some piece of the federal monopoly, and mandates that take away citizens' rights. Despite the best of intentions, this program failed under its own weight.

One simple option is for the government to pay for the policies, at a cost of $30 billion to $50 billion. Alternatively, the government can implement federal and state risk pools to spread costs between the insurer, the patient, and the government. Either way, the needed legislation requires only a handful of pages.

Two packages of goodies—the Cornhusker Kickback (Nebraska) and the Louisiana Purchase—were crafted to buy the votes needed to pass the ACA in the Senate, and misdirected millions of taxpayer dollars away from anything having to do with the public's health and well-being.

The Chief Simplicity Office will upgrade the legislative branch to Congress 2.0, expanding the sourcing of ideas beyond traditional special interests to involve innovators from across the country, from university students and professors to interested citizens. Awarding an X-Prize to outsiders will accelerate innovative solutions not likely to come from the last-century status quo.

In 2016, the Competitive Research Institute estimated the cost of compliance with the increasing number of regulations at $2 trillion, or about 11 percent of the economy. The last couple of years, that number has dropped to $1.85 trillion, or 8.5 percent of GDP. This percentage would likely go back up under a different president and political party, as there is no institution for simplifying regulation.

For the government to be effective, its scope should be well defined, with the smartest, leanest, best run footprint so that it can once again be a good administrator. The Chief Simplicity Office is one of seven government innovations that will deliver a less expensive, more effective government that is easier to manage and lead. And easier for the voter to understand.

#7 CIVIL: Immigration for the Twenty-First Century

Top Priority: High-Value Tech and Life Science Entrepreneurs

At the beginning of the nineteenth century, immigration was free and open. America had a vast landmass to fill, and 'farmer' was the number one job description. America's doors were wide open for anyone with a strong back and a will to own their own land. After World War II, immigration of extremely high value talent from around the world rose dramatically because the United States was the 'best game in town.' Left unravaged by the war and with the largest, freest economy in the world, we were a magnet for the best of the best.

In the twenty-first century, our requirements are vastly different than they were in 1800 or 1900 or even 1980. The need for immigrants with no education, no skills and little or no experience is long past. In this century automation and robotics will reduce the need for low- or no-skills jobs unlike the twentieth century, when industry automated new industries rose. Farming jobs, once ninety percent of our economy, fell to a few percent while industrial and manufacturing jobs skyrocketed. When automation arrived in these industries, the information technology industry flourished, as did the need for highly skilled workers. This trend will continue this century. Retail jobs have diminished while online shopping has skyrocketed. The needs of the economy are also changing more rapidly. The typical Fortune 500 company from the early twentieth century lasted one hundred years. Today's expected longevity is only nineteen years. The trend for new jobs is an ever-increasing need for highly skilled workers. Even shop floor workers in a factory need to be familiar with the automation that runs the machinery.

Encouraging low- or no-skills immigration only assures that these immigrants will shortly be competing with intelligent robots for jobs. This would be both mean to the immigrants and ineffective with respect to economic growth. The competition for the highly educated and high-tech entrepreneurs is vastly greater today than last century.

Our highest priorities this century center on ideas, inventions, and innovation. These are the economic currency of success this century. They translate into two key priorities: 1) entrepreneurs, especially those in life sciences and technology among others, and 2) highly educated immigrants in the hard sciences like physics, chemistry, engineering genomic engineering and the like. Though America has always done well in these areas, we need to step up our efforts to compete with China's thirty-year plan to kick America and western civilization to the curb. Our competitive advantage to get these high value immigrants after World War II was the fact that there really was nowhere else to immigrate. America was the land of opportunity, and the devasting effects of the war did not reach our shores. There simply was not a better place to renew one's life.

214 | CAPITALISM, SOCIALISM, AND DEMOCRACY

This century is vastly more economically competitive. Dozens of industrialized nations have a great foundation to launch a new business. Sound economies with high economic freedom indexes have made them more competitive in attracting entrepreneurial immigrants. Staying in one's home country, especially when their economic freedom index is high, means it may be just as easy to launch an international business without moving. Additionally, vast swaths of private capital that have shifted to China are capturing new entrepreneurs. Our economy needs faster growth than the 2.5 percent average over the last twenty years if America is to keep China's economic growth and girth at bay.

During the twentieth century America's high economic freedom was a magnet for immigrant entrepreneurs. In 2019, *Newsweek* touted that 45 percent of the Fortune 500 were founded by immigrants or the children of immigrants. As private capital flows to other nations like China and other emerging economies, the challenge for attracting entrepreneurs will be much more competitive. To accelerate economic growth, the two top priorities start with entrepreneurs and the highly educated, especially those who are seeking to patent discoveries or are doing research in technology (especially AI and Machine Learning) and life sciences. Quotas for these immigrants are not needed.

One crucial step is required before a new immigration policy is possible. Every elected official in the United States, from dog catcher to president, needs to retake their oath of office to enforce the laws of the nation, from local to federal. Although the current immigration laws may leave much to be desired, their enforcement is essential. If our local, state, and federal leaders opt out of enforcing our laws, the rule of law falters and dies, and so too does the voters' trust in government. Once we agree to enforce laws, creating a new structure is possible. Without this step in the process, all political negotiations are just partisan gaming designed to raise money, not improve the results of our economic and social ventures.

Proposed Immigration Structure Allows the Following:

- Persons who will invest or have investment above $200,000 in a job-creating enterprise that employs at least one full time U.S. worker, or persons that have a business idea, research proposal or pending patent. Unlimited access until annual new business formation exceeds 750,000 annually (adjusted up annually as percentage increase in population.) Top priorities: technology and life sciences. Country by country limits are recommended to assure that the effects of talent drain of immigrating nations is minimized.

- Persons of extraordinary ability in the arts, science, education, business, or athletics; outstanding professors and researchers, multinational executives, and managers. 80,000

- Special needs for skilled occupations without talent pool: Example: The U.S. previously had a shortage of welders. Numbers should be defined annually as needs will change rapidly.

- Members of the professions holding advanced degrees, or persons of exceptional abilities in the arts, science, engineering, or business. 80,000

- Certain "special immigrants" including religious workers, employees of U.S. foreign service posts, former U.S. government employees and other classes of aliens. 10,000

- Immediate relatives of U.S. Citizens, wives/husbands, and children: and entrepreneurs represented in the first bullet item above.

- Temporary Worker Program: To be measured by annual need by industries affected. Industries such as hospitality and farm workers should be accommodated by our immigration policy.

- Refugees: Maintain status.

- End Chain Migration/Family Unification except for immediate family (spouse and children).

Regarding the technology industry and H1-B visas. America needs to take great care to assure that these visas are not at the expense of American jobs. A few years ago, Disney acquired visas for Information Technology workers, which could be fine, except for the fact the new hires were replacing the entire IT staff. More humiliating, the IT staff had to train the new H1-B new hires. This conduct is unacceptable and cannot be part of any visa process. Period.

The road to economic success in the twenty-first century is directly in proportion to the generation of innovations, ideas, and inventions. When international entrepreneurs bring their ideas to the U.S. to create businesses, they increase business formation and expand employment. When America focuses on high-value persons in research, science, engineering and more, this expands the talent pool required to support the growth of these new twenty-first century businesses and complements the growth of businesses that already reside in the U.S. These two areas should be our highest priorities with our new immigration policy.

In 2016, China produced one million new patents and one million new businesses. Though reporting from China is seldom accurate, these numbers are double U.S. numbers, and we need to be conscious of the fact that these variables are central to economic growth in the twenty-first century.

Economist William Easterly noted that idea generation is proportional to a nation's population. China has four times the capacity for idea generation versus America because it has four times the population. America needs to maximize its efforts for creating ideas and then bolster those numbers with increased economic freedom and private investment to assure the highest number of good ideas make it to market. This holistic growth can then be complimented by immigration focused on new businesses and new jobs.

Our current immigration system, even if merit requirements by the Trump administration are added, will not be able to overcome China's growth plan, the mission of which is designed to displace the U.S. in the number one economy, and to use their new economic power to kick the U.S. and Western approach to economic and political freedom to the curb.

A more focused immigration policy will help assure this does not happen.

#8 CIVIL: Health care for the Twenty-First Century

Top Priority: Plan for your health to reduce costs!

During the last few election cycles, the rhetoric surrounding the cost of health insurance quickly devolved into bromides and sound bites about protecting or defending big government health programs. Washington elites make promises that never quite meet expectations but make for great Madison Avenue advertising.

There are three key reasons for the high cost of health insurance, 1) the HMO/PPO is the most expensive solution for financing health care, 2) each year 5 percent of the patients produce 50 percent of the costs, and 3) our health care is a lifetime process, and our insurance policy is non-portable and an annual event.

Health Financing as a Lifetime Challenge

In 2004, the *National Center for Biotechnology Information* published *The Lifetime Distribution of Health Care Costs*. Average lifetime costs in 2000 dollars totaled $316,000, about $480,000 in 2020 dollars. The percentage of lifetime costs by age:

- Birth to nineteen years—7.8 percent.
- Twenty to thirty-nine years—12.5 percent.
- Forty to sixty-four years—31 percent.
- Over sixty-five years—48.6 percent.

Were insurance policy terms decades long instead of a single year, the cost of coverage would be greatly diminished. The HMO/PPO is both an annual health insurance that we all use (legislated into our lives during the Nixon Administration with insights from insurer Kaiser Permanente) and covers every health event in a person's life from sniffles to a heart transplant. It is the *most expensive solution* possible for insuring health care.

The cost of a typical policy for a family of four is $1,000 per month, split between the employee and the employer. Policy costs rise or fall based on co-pays and deductibles. In terms of worker pay, the $1000 per month insurance bill translates to $6 an hour. Fifty percent of Americans earn less than $16 an hour. For these workers, a thousand-dollar monthly premium is unaffordable, for both the employee and employer. For part-time workers earning $10 an hour, the financial challenge is even greater. For single men or women in their twenties having to provide their own insurance, who were mandated to purchase insurance under the Affordable Care Act, the average monthly cost for a high deductible policy, $200 per month, was out of reach and many opted to be taxed. Because the young have less perception of need or risk, any expense for medical coverage may seem unreasonable.

Annual Versus Lifetime

For almost everyone, as we age, there is increasing likelihood of expensive health care expenses whether from disease or end-of-life expenses.

If you go to work in an office of twenty people, one person will have a health event that costs over $100,000 and potentially over $250,000. If you and your employer pay $1000 for your coverage, $500 of the premium goes to pay the expenses of that one person. The person with an expensive health care problem changes each year. There is, though, no planning, no saving, for this expensive health event though we all know it is coming at some point in our lives, generally after forty.

The HMO/PPO isn't going away, and should not, but better options—more affordable options—are needed, options that consider that health care costs can be planned for, especially because four-fifths of health care costs occur after age forty and can be saved for during our teens, twenties, and thirties, mitigating the risk of high costs with a longer-term insurance instrument.

The Whole Health – Health Savings Account – Prepaid Credit Card – Building Block Insurance Policy

A longer-term insurance policy will provide much needed cost relief, especially for those from eighteen to forty, because risk is spread over decades instead of from year to year. The longer the policy term, the better. Workers seeking their first job could invest in a fifty-year policy. Shorter term policies for thirty-, forty-, and fifty-year-olds are also financially feasible.

What are the features of this new policy approach? First, it needs to act like a cross between a Whole Life insurance and Term Insurance policy. Whole Life and Term Insurance policies pay the face value upon death. Whole Life policies also have a cash value which grows over time. Whole Health Insurance would have both benefits with a designated cash value at the end of the policy based on any residual value at the end of the term.

Second, the best usage of Whole Health is for major health costs. The policy could be used like a Health Savings Account to pay for minor health events, or for premium payments if the policy holder is out of work. Another great benefit is that the policy holder can replenish the account to maintain its value.

Third, whole health policies could be purchased in blocks with the ability to increase the value of the policy when risks and needs increase, especially as income increases, and, most importantly, when marriage and family increase the need to protect against financial risk from health issues.

Catastrophic insurance should be an add-on. If the $10,000 deductible policy for a single twenty-one-year-old is about $200 a month, catastrophic coverage for $250,000 (what a married person with children should have today) would likely be $20 per month or less. For families, this option would be a natural add-on.

A starter policy of $25,000 is not unreasonable. If death rates for Life Insurance policies align with big health costs, the actuarial estimates for Whole Life Insurance Policies are about $25 per month. This is a fraction of the cost of an HMO/PPO.

With a Whole Health Policy, a business seeking to provide benefits for workers who earn less than $15 an hour could split the premium with the worker or pay 100 percent with assistance from the government for low-income families. A Health Savings Account could be funded as well. The cost of Whole Health pricing comes in at $.30 an hour for a full-time worker and $.50 for a part-time worker working twenty-four hours a week. At these rates, every business can afford to offer affordable health coverage to younger new hires and workers through age fifty. This solution could also compliment government programs like Medicaid and Obamacare.

The biggest benefit is that neither the government nor the health insurance companies will be telling you how to spend your dollars unless your costs require dipping into the catastrophic coverage. Second, this solution has no deductible or co-pays. Third, the cost of insurance makes it affordable for every worker/business right down to minimum wage workers. Finally, health care moves to a cash business which will create a downward pressure on pricing.

Whole Life Insurance should be considered one of many solutions provided by an open and freer market. The more options and competition, the more likely the needs of patient financing will be served from rich to poor.

Beyond Financing

Congress and the health care marketplace *must* improve pricing transparency. The patient has no idea what an office visit costs much less a specific drug or a heart transplant. To do this, our patient experience needs a twenty-first century face. Look at www.kbb.com. For car buyers, the *Kelly Blue*

Book anonymizes car purchase data across the nation and provides the user an estimate range of prices for model, make, year by zip code. Finding a way to do the same for health care costs for doctors, hospitals, and pharma would do worlds of good to supplement our decision making.

Health Care Background: Future Trends.

The trend of personalized, genomic health care needs to be taken into consideration regarding new solutions for health care financing.

The life sciences and health care markets have two evolving price curves that are peaking. The first price curve arrives from traditional—or analog— medical innovation like the next new imaging technology or a one-size fits-all drug that helps increase the life span of a cancer patient but does not cure the patient. The cost of these traditional innovations has tended to increase time. These innovations are not unlike innovations in the car industry. Electric door locks, air conditioning, navigation systems and safety devices produce a higher quality automobile, but also a more expensive one.

The second price curve developing around personalized, genomic medicine will deliver a price curve more like a computer chip. Over time the chip has become more powerful and less expensive. For genomic medicine—a personalized medicine—the price curve will be much the same, as new pharma solutions are made for the individual patient and will cure patients of a disease using DNA as a programming language—a new digital domain for medicine.

How are these two vastly dissimilar kinds of medicine different in terms of costs?

Today, if you are feeling ill, a trip to the general practitioner may produce a recommendation to see an oncologist. A likely follow-up will find you at the hospital for a biopsy. A positive test results in surgery which requires a surgeon, nurses, an anesthesiologist and an expensive operating room. A few days in recovery in the hospital is followed by chemotherapy and additional visits to the oncologist and a menu of pharma to assist in recovery as well as anti-cancer drugs to reduce the possibility of the cancer's recurrence. The accumulated costs for all these professionals and a sterile environment for surgery and recovery costs on average above $150,000. With all the people and resources required, the costs are easy to understand.

Genomic toolkits for editing our DNA will likely make this expensive scenario obsolete. Cures will be 'made to order' from reprogramming your broken DNA. Personized medicine will revolutionize medicine in two ways, 1) curatives will be made specifically for one person and the effectiveness of the pharma will be near 100 percent, and 2) according to one CEO, manufacturing costs for this solution will be cut 2000 times over today's pharma. Building pharma plants for current drugs costs a billion dollars to make just one drug. Future personalized pharma can make innumerable pharmaceutics in the same plant at scale.

This new approach will be akin to the science fiction of the 1960s *Star Trek*. Dr. McCoy waved a tricorder over the patient and, with a curious eye, reviewed the results. In the back-room lab, he manufactured the cure and then injected it into the patient. Voila, a healed patient. Our future health care will mimic this scenario.

Today, personalized medicine is new. Its costs, like any new technology, are high. The numbers of genomic health solutions and cures are beginning to accelerate. Sometime near mid-century, expect personalized cures will begin to commoditize with costs floating down to generic drug pricing. This new approach will dramatically reduce the costs of health care and turn our sick care system into a health care system.

With health care remedies increasing and with short term policies term that cover literally everything, is there a better solution, or set of solutions to provide options to workers?

Government solutions, though, have consistently constricted health financing options and delivered steadily rising prices. The government's only tools to reign in the cost of insurance are price fixing or negotiating large-scale contracts that produce some reductions in cost. Both have limits that quickly can impair quality care and diminish access to services.

For example, those who tout they will protect or defend Medicare rely on reduced payouts for medical services and pharma and have little room left to cut prices. In *Wall Street Journal,* authors Benedic Ippolito and Chris Pope wrote that, "Hospitals now are effectively required to treat Medicare enrollees at rates averaging 59 percent less than what hospitals receive from employer-sponsored insurance plans." Artificially reducing these costs for Medicare patients drives up costs for the 150,000,000 people with private insurance which does not solve the overall expense challenge. A typical worker cannot work for 59 percent less wages; nor can a business take 59 percent less for their products.

Ask any business how long they will be in operation if customers paid only 41 percent of the list price. Answer is, "Not long." As the population ages, the mix of patients for providers rises, tilting toward the aged. If private insurance disappeared, the medical system would crash. There is some room to artificially lower prices, but not much. There are better places to look for relief.

Better understanding of why premiums have continually risen is essential to finding solutions that will reduce insurance costs. Four key challenging areas create constantly increasing premiums: 1) the only insurance coverage available, the HMO/PPO, is the most expensive possible solution for health care financing which is great for insurance companies but not the policy holders, 2) health insurance is provided as an annual policy and health care is a lifetime challenge with costs increasing with age, 3) 5 percent of patients accrue 50 percent of the health care costs each year and, therefore, contribute 50 percent to the cost of every policy holder's premium, and 4) new medical innovations are added to plans each year increasing costs of insurance policies.

Finally, when genomic health does finally commoditize near mid-century and reduce the cost of health care, Whole Life Policies will likely cover future health expense for the Medicare years, too, reducing the reliance of our future elders on Medicare.

#9 The Onramp to Twenty-First Century Federal Superstructure
Moving State, Local and Federal Technology into the Digital Century

There is no doubt that transportation infrastructure needs an update due to the lack of investment made by state, local, and federal governments over the past few decades. Given the federal government's mediocre stewardship of our federal highway tax dollars, and the states' different needs and variable maintenance and construction costs, responsibilities for revenue, maintenance, and construction should move back to the states. This is the best allocation of capital.

A more important infrastructure project lies with Information Technology. The federal technology infrastructure is even worse than our roads. The federal government needs to ramp up its schedule and budget to engage in the digital economy. States, counties, and cities share the problem of aging hardware and software.

CIVIL recommends, first, getting systems up to date by finding new solutions and retiring old, on premise, custom solutions, and solutions based on technology that is no longer upgradeable. Second, find solutions that are engineered for cloud technology, which is much easier to scale. Finally, invest heavily in technology that can deliver real time analytics, or near real time. Focus on typical data-driven analytics, but ensure that analytic solutions embed predictive capabilities, machine learning, text analysis, geospatial components, and social media analysis. Additionally, use customer experience data to leverage both worker and citizen input about the quality and usefulness of the solutions.

The government isn't deaf to these needs, but investments in new technology have been on the wane and many implementations are behind schedule, meaning that the government is outside the innovation loop. Technology transformations are a challenge for any business, small or large. For the federal government, which spends nearly $100 billion annually, mostly on keeping its existing technology running, making the leap into twenty-first century computing is a vast but vital goal. The cost of keeping old, often kludgy systems functioning guarantees high maintenance and operating costs. It also deprives government of the agility and flexibility required to run a great nation. When business technology lags, poor governance in not far behind, and the enterprise generally winds up on the economic trash heap. Our government technology gap, like that of any business, is a heavy tax on our nation's productivity.

According to Nextgov.com, "One of the IRS' most important tax-processing applications is old enough to be a grandparent, and officials warn a failure during tax season could have dire economic ramifications or delay tax refunds for 100 million Americans. ... Despite hundreds of millions in spending, plans to fully modernize the application are more than six years behind schedule, and in a statement to Nextgov, IRS revised its new timeline for a modernized IMF to 2022."

Imagine that similar problems exist across the more than 400 departments, agencies, and sub-agencies, 50 states, 3000 counties, and 20,000 incorporated cities.

Moving to a digital government is a continual endeavor. While federal, state, and local governments are making an effort, they need to implement technology improvements and whole-scale upgrades across all departments. Mounting large-scale, effective responses to national disasters, like the Covid-19 pandemic, depends on it. Government's role in supporting private sector innovation depends on it. Running, maintaining, and defending our country depends on it.

The federal government has produced a general plan for use of cloud solutions. What is missing is 1) a priority list for which agencies will acquire the most benefit from cloud transformations and 2) the budget that funds the projects. Last year, only $5.4 billion of the government's $100 billion budget was allocated to the cloud. According to Deltek, this number will only increase to $9.1 billion by 2024. This increase is tiny compared to budgets to fund major transformations at the federal level. The first two steps to aggressively attacking the laggard systems are 1) prioritize the solutions that produce the most return on investment, and 2) outline the expected investments required to update these solutions.

What is the size of a transformational budget? Something in the range of three to ten times the current budget. Add more for a complete redo of all systems. The payback, however, would be extraordinary. Imagine if voters and our leaders could understand within months where a proposed program met its objectives, and if not, what the potential challenges were so that it could be fixed. Envision a solution where voters could track capital projects in real time so we could monitor progress, or lack thereof. Imagine a government that needs fewer people to maintain aging software that can now be deployed to manage government's key process indicators. Imagine reasonable budgets for upgrading system software to the newest version (with new benefits), and upgrades that are mostly automated. And imagine new solutions that provide the advantages of machine learning, text analysis, and voter experience software to better understand our needs and preferences.

The possibilities are endless with a transformation to digital government. Execution requires a plan with priorities and budget, and the will of the people and our leaders.

#10 Space: A National Goal and Common Vision

Not Only Good for the Economy, a Goal That Can Bring Us Together!
Space: A National Goal and Common Vision

According to a Pew Research report from June 6, 2018, just over 70 percent of Americans want the U.S. to continue leading the world in space exploration, and 80 percent believe the space station is a great idea. But space exploration not only thrills the American imagination, it offers a big financial payback. According to *The Conversation* in 2014, "For every US$1 put into the US space agency, its citizens get US$10 as payback." The payback comes from technologies born from aerospace research and development, including the microwave, GPS, artificial limbs, and solar cells.

Manned space missions were grounded following the explosion of the Space Shuttle Challenger in 1986. In 2019, the Air Force Space Command, created in 1982, became the United States Space Force, established by the 2020 National Defense Authorization Act to provide space-based defense, with formal plans to return to the moon and venture to Mars. However, the budgets for these new endeavors are meek. Since topping out in the 1960s at 4 percent of the federal budget, NASA spending declined to 1 percent in the 1970s—1980s to a low of .5 percent during the last decade. As the competition, especially from China, gets aggressive, we need longer-term, more visionary goals.

Budgets were less of a challenge in 1960, when only 22 percent of the budget went to social programs, whereas social programs, which now account for almost 67 percent of the budget, crowd out other investments. CIVIL programs that promote for smart, streamlined government can create budget savings that allow for better investments in government-sponsored economic productivity.

Increased budgets will speed up the timelines of our space ventures and help fund longer term goals beyond Mars. Research in deep space propulsion will also align with energy research for advanced clean energy solutions that include nuclear, fusion, and anti-matter propulsion.

Missions to the asteroid belts and two of the solar system's icy moons—Jupiter's Europa, and Saturn's Enceladus, which may contain life—and deep space flight are the key components for our long-range plans. Early deep space flight will not only use new propulsion technologies; artificial intelligence will allow for long journeys of more than a century to investigate potentially habitable planets.

Space is not just about technology revelations or scientific endeavor; it is humanity's ticket to permanence in our galaxy by being explorers of the solar system, our galaxy, and the universe. Innovation and new technologies over the last four hundred years have answered humanity's basic needs. If our focus becomes too earth focused, the likely end game is human extinction.

The biggest short-term benefit is promoting a common goal and century-long roadmap that we can all get behind, that we can learn from, and that produces economic benefit for everyone, not just Americans, but citizens worldwide.

Conclusion

These ten planks provide a new platform for evidence-based governance, the most important feature of which may be the American Success Dashboard that provides visibility for every American into the results of each program, or, for that matter, any and every program and dollar spent by the government. Our lack of visibility has allowed political parties and their press adherents to spin results. The voter is left in the blind without a single trusted source of the truth.

Most important, evidence-based government integrates the best of democratic Capitalism's idea engine, optimizing *ideas having sex with ideas* as well as improving outcomes for the occasionally required social monopoly when needed and—when results don't match objectives—a path to an exit or a transformation.

Citizen feedback is welcomed at tom@civilgovernance.org.

www.ingramcontent.com/pod-product-compliance
Lightning Source LLC
Chambersburg PA
CBHW052127270326
41930CB00012B/2790